Humorous Stories of HENRY LAWSON

Humorous Stories of HENRY LAWSON

Decorated with watercolours and sketches
by S. T. Gill

ANGUS
& ROBERTSON
PUBLISHERS

ACKNOWLEDGEMENTS

Unless otherwise stated, all works by S. T. Gill
are reproduced by permission of the Mitchell
Library, State Library of New South Wales.

ANGUS & ROBERTSON PUBLISHERS

*Unit 4, Eden Park, 31 Waterloo Road,
North Ryde, NSW, Australia 2113; and
16 Golden Square, London W1R 4BN,
United Kingdom*

*First published in Australia
by Angus & Robertson Publishers in 1987
Reprinted in 1989*

Copyright © Angus & Robertson 1987

*National Library of Australia
Cataloguing-in-publication data.*

*Lawson, Henry, 1867-1922.
  Humorous stories of Henry Lawson.
  ISBN 0 207 15511 9.
  I. Mann, Cecil, 1896-1967. II. Title.
A823'.2*

*Typeset in 10pt Goudy Old Style
Printed in Hong Kong*

5   4   3   2

93   92   91   90   89

CONTENTS

Stiffner and Jim

(THIRDLY, BILL)

WE were tramping down in Canterbury, Maoriland, at the time, swagging it—me and Bill—looking for work on the new railway-line. Well, one afternoon, after a long, hot tramp, we comes to Stiffner's Hotel—between Christchurch and that other place—I forget the name of it—with throats on us like sunstruck bones, and not the price of a stick of tobacco.

We had to have a drink, anyway, so we chanced it. We walked right into the bar, handed over our swags, put up four drinks, and tried to look as if we'd just drawn our cheques and didn't care a curse for any man. We looked solvent enough, as far as swagmen go. We were dirty and haggard and ragged and tired-looking, and that was all the more reason why we might have our cheques all right.

This Stiffner was a hard customer. He'd been a spieler, fighting man, bush parson, temperance preacher, and a policeman, and a commercial traveller, and everything else that was damnable; he'd been a journalist, and an editor; he'd been a lawyer, too. He was an ugly brute to look at, and uglier to have a row with—about six-foot-six, wide in proportion and stronger than Donald Dinnie.

He was meaner than a goldfield Chinaman, and sharper than a sewer rat: he wouldn't give his own father a feed, nor lend him a sprat—unless some safe person backed the old man's I.O.U.

We knew that we needn't expect any mercy from Stiffner; but something had to be done, so I said to Bill:

"Something's got to be done, Bill! What do you think of it?"

Bill was mostly a quiet young chap, from Sydney, except when he got drunk—which was seldom—and then he was a lively customer from all round. He was cracked on the subject of spielers. He held that the population of the world was divided into two classes—one was spielers and the other was mugs. He reckoned that he wasn't a mug. At first I thought that he was a spieler, and afterwards I thought that he was a mug. He used to say that a man had

1

to do it these times; that he was honest once and a fool, and was robbed and starved in consequence by his friends and relations; but now he intended to take all that he could get. He said that you either had to have or be had; that men were driven to be sharps, and there was no help for it.

Bill said:

"We'll have to sharpen our teeth, that's all, and chew somebody's lug."

"How?" I asked.

There was a lot of navvies at the pub, and I knew one or two by sight, so Bill says:

"You know one or two of these mugs. Bite one of their ears."

So I took aside a chap that I knowed and bit his ear for ten bob, and gave it to Bill to mind, for I thought it would be safer with him than with me.

"Hang on to that," I says, "and don't lose it for your natural life's sake, or Stiffner'll stiffen us."

We put up about nine bob's worth of drinks that night—me and Bill—and Stiffner didn't squeal: he was too sharp. He shouted once or twice.

By and by I left Bill and turned in, and in the morning when I woke up there was Bill sitting alongside of me, and looking about as lively as the fighting kangaroo in London in fog-time. He had a black eye and eighteen pence. He'd been taking down some of the mugs.

"Well, what's to be done now?" I asked. "Stiffner can smash us both with one hand, and if we don't pay up he'll pound our swags and cripple us. He's just the man to do it. He loves a fight even more than he hates being had."

"There's only one thing to be done, Jim," says Bill, in a tired, disinterested tone that made me mad.

"Well, what's that?" I said.

"Smoke!"

"Smoke be damned," I snarled, losing my temper. "You know dashed well that our swags are in the bar, and we can't smoke without them."

"Well, then," says Bill, "I'll toss you to see who's to face the landlord."

"Well, I'll be blessed!" I says. "I'll see you further first. You have got a front. You mugged that stuff away, and you'll have to get us out of the mess."

It made him wild to be called a mug, and we swore and growled at each other for a while; but we daren't speak loud enough to have a fight, so at last I agreed to toss up for it, and I lost.

Bill started to give me some of his points, but I shut him up quick.

"You've had your turn, and made a mess of it," I said. "For God's sake give me a show. Now, I'll go into the bar and ask for the swags, and carry them out on to the veranda, and then go back to settle up. You keep him talking all the time. You dump the two swags together, and smoke like sheol. That's all you've got to do."

I went into the bar, got the swags from the missus, carried them out on to the veranda, and then went back.

Stiffner came in.

"Good morning!"

"Good morning, sir," says Stiffner.

"It'll be a nice day, I think?"

"Yes, I think so. I suppose you are going on?"

"Yes, we'll have to make a move today." Then I hooked carelessly on to the counter with one elbow, and looked dreary-like out across the clearing, and presently I gave a sort of sigh and said: "Ah, well! I think I'll have a beer."

"Right you are! Where's your mate?"

"Oh, he's round at the back. He'll be round directly; but he ain't drinking this morning."

Stiffner laughed that nasty empty laugh of his. He thought Bill was whipping the cat.

"What's yours, boss?" I said.

"Thankee. . . . Here's luck!"

"Here's luck!"

The country was pretty open round there—the nearest timber was better than a mile away, and I wanted to give Bill a good start across the flat before the go-as-you-can commenced; so I talked for a while, and while we were talking I thought I might as well go the whole hog—I might as well die for a pound as a penny, if I had to die; and if I hadn't I'd have the pound to the good, anyway, so to speak. Anyhow, the risk would be about the same, or less, for I might have the spirit to run harder the more I had to run for—the more spirits I had to run for, in fact, as it turned out—so I says:

3

"I think I'll take one of them there flasks of whisky to last us on the road."

"Right y'are," says Stiffner. "What'll yer have—a small one or a big one?"

"Oh, a big one, I think—if I can get it into my pocket."

"It'll be a tight squeeze," he said, and he laughed.

"I'll try," I said. "Bet you two drinks I'll get it in."

"Done!" he says. "The top inside coat-pocket, and no tearing."

It was a big bottle, and all my pockets were small; but I got it into the pocket he'd betted against. It was a tight squeeze, but I got it in.

Then we both laughed, but his laugh was nastier than usual, because it was meant to be pleasant, and he'd lost two drinks; and my laugh wasn't easy—I was anxious as to which of us would laugh next.

Just then I noticed something, and an idea struck me—about the most up-to-date idea that ever struck me in my life. I noticed that Stiffner was limping on his right foot this morning, so I said to him:

"What's up with your foot?" putting my hand in my pocket.

"Oh, it's a crimson nail in my boot," he said. "I thought I got the blanky thing out this morning; but I didn't."

There just happened to be an old bag of shoemaker's tools in the bar, belonging to an old cobbler who was lying dead drunk on the veranda. So I said, taking my hand out of my pocket again:

"Lend us the boot, and I'll fix it in a minute. That's my old trade."

"Oh, so you're a shoemaker," he said. "I'd never have thought it."

He laughs one of his useless laughs that wasn't wanted, and slips off the boot—he hadn't laced it up—and hands it across the bar to me. It was an ugly brute—a great thick, iron-bound, boiler-plated navvy's boot. It made me feel sore when I looked at it.

I got the bag and pretended to fix the nail; but I didn't.

"There's a couple of nails gone from the sole," I said. "I'll put 'em in if I can find any hobnails, and it'll save the sole," and I rooted in the bag and found a good long nail, and shoved it right through the sole on the sly. He'd been a bit of a sprinter in his time, and I thought it might be better for me in the near future if the spikes of his running-shoes were inside.

"There, you'll find that better, I fancy," I said, standing the boot on the bar counter, but keeping my hand on it in an absent-minded kind of way. Presently I yawned and stretched myself, and said in a careless way:

"Ah, well! How's the slate?"

He scratched the back of his head and pretended to think.

"Oh, well, we'll call it thirty bob."

Perhaps he thought I'd slap down two quid.

"Well," I says, "and what will you do supposing we don't pay you?"

He looked blank for a moment. Then he fired up and gasped and choked once or twice; and then he cooled down suddenly and laughed his nastiest laugh—he was one of those men who always laugh when they're wild—and said in a nasty, quiet tone:

"You thundering, jumped-up crawlers! If you don't (something) well part up I'll take your swags and (something) well kick your gory pants so you won't be able to sit down for a month—or stand up either!"

"Well, the sooner you begin the better," I said; and I chucked the boot into a corner and bolted.

He jumped the bar counter, got his boot, and came after me. He paused to slip the boot on—but he only made one step, and then gave a howl and slung the boot off and rushed back. When I looked round again he'd got a slipper on, and was coming—and gaining on me, too. I shifted scenery pretty quick the next five minutes. But I was soon pumped. My heart began to beat against the ceiling of my head, and my lungs all choked up in my throat. When I guessed he was getting within kicking distance I glanced round so's to dodge the kick. He let out; but I shied just in time. He missed fire, and the slipper went about twenty feet up in the air and fell in a waterhole.

He was done then, for the ground was stubbly and stony. I seen Bill on ahead pegging out for the horizon, and I took after him and reached for the timber for all I was worth, for I'd seen Stiffner's missus coming with a shovel—to bury the remains, I suppose; and those two were a good match—Stiffner and his missus, I mean.

Bill looked round once, and melted into the bush pretty soon after that. When I caught up he was about done; but I grabbed my swag and we pushed on, for I told Bill that I'd seen Stiffner making for the stables when I'd last looked round; and Bill thought that we'd better get lost in the bush as soon as ever we could, and stay lost, too, for Stiffner was a man that couldn't stand being had.

The first thing that Bill said when we got safe into camp was: "I told you that we'd pull through all right. You need never be frightened when you're travelling with me. Just take my advice and leave things to me, and we'll hang out all right. Now——"

But I shut him up. He made me mad.

"Why, you ——! What the sheol did *you* do?"

"Do?" he says. "I got away with the swags, didn't I? Where'd they be now if it wasn't for me?"

Then I sat on him pretty hard for his pretensions, and paid him out for all the patronage he'd worked off on me, and called him a mug straight, and walked round him, so to speak, and blowed, and told him never to pretend to me again that he was a battler.

Then, when I thought I'd licked him into form, I cooled down and soaped him up a bit; but I never thought that he had three climaxes and a crisis in store for me.

He took it all pretty cool; he let me have my fling, and gave me time to get breath; then he leaned languidly over on his right side, shoved his left hand down into his left trouser-pocket, and brought up a bootlace, a box of matches, and nine-and-six.

As soon as I got the focus of it I gasped:

"Where the deuce did you get that?"

"I had it all along," he said, "but I seen at the pub that you had the show to chew a lug, so I thought we'd save it—nine-and-sixpences ain't picked up every day."

Then he leaned over on his left, went down into the other pocket, and came up with a piece of tobacco and half a sovereign. My eyes bulged out.

"Where the blazes did you get that from?" I yelled.

"That," he said, "was the half-quid you give me last night. Half-quids ain't to be thrown away these times; and, besides, I had a down on Stiffner, and meant to pay him out; I reckoned that if we wasn't sharp enough to take him down we hadn't any business to be supposed to be alive. Anyway, I guessed we'd do it; and so we did—and got a bottle of whisky into the bargain."

Then he leaned back, tired-like, against the log, and dredged his upper left-hand waistcoat-pocket, and brought up a sovereign wrapped in a pound note. Then he waited for me to speak; but I couldn't. I got my mouth open, but couldn't get it shut again.

"I got that out of the mugs last night, but I thought that we'd want it, and might as well keep it. Quids ain't so easily picked up, nowadays; and, besides, we need stuff more'n Stiffner does, and so——"

"And did he know you had the stuff?" I gasped.

"Oh, yes, that's the fun of it. That's what made him so excited. He was in the parlour all the time I was playing. But we might as well have a drink!"

We did. I wanted it.

Bill turned in by and by, and looked like a sleeping innocent in the moonlight. I sat up late, and smoked, and thought hard, and watched Bill, and turned in, and thought till near daylight, and then went to sleep, and had a nightmare about it. I dreamed I chased Stiffner forty miles to buy his pub, and that Bill turned out to be his nephew.

Bill divvied up all right, and gave me half a crown over, but I didn't travel with him long after that. He was a decent young fellow as far as chaps go, and a good mate as far as mates go; but he was too far ahead for a peaceful, easygoing chap like me. It would have worn me out in a year to keep up to him.

The Ironbark Chip

DAVE REGAN and party—bush-fencers, tank-sinkers, and rough carpenters—were finishing the third and last culvert of their contract on the last section of the new railway-line, and had already sent in their vouchers for the completed contract, so that there might be no excuse for extra delay in connection with the cheque.

Now it had been expressly stipulated in the plans and specifications that the timber for certain beams and girders was to be ironbark and no other, and government inspectors were authorized to order the removal from the ground of any timber or material they might deem inferior, or not in accordance with the stipulations. The railway contractor's foreman and inspector of sub-contractors was a practical man and a bushman, but he had been a timbergetter himself; his sympathies were bushy, and he was on winking terms with Dave Regan. Besides, extended time was expiring, and the contractors were in a hurry to complete the line. But the government inspector was a reserved man who poked round on his independent own and appeared in lonely spots at unexpected times—with apparently no definite object in life—like a grey kangaroo bothered by a new wire fence, but unsuspicious of the presence of humans. He wore a grey suit, rode, or mostly led, an ashen-grey horse; the grass was long and grey, so he was seldom spotted until he was well within the horizon and bearing leisurely down on a party of sub-contractors, leading his horse.

Now, ironbark was scarce and distant on those ridges, and another timber, similar in appearance, but much inferior in grain and "standing" quality, was plentiful and close at hand. Dave and party were "about full of" the job and place, and wanted to get their cheque and be gone to another "spec" they had in view. So they came to reckon they'd get the last girder from a handy tree, and have it squared, in place, and carefully and conscientiously tarred before the inspector happened along, if he did. But they didn't. They got it squared, and ready to be lifted into its place; the kindly darkness of tar was ready to cover a fraud that took four strong men with crowbars and levers to shift; and now (such is the regular cussedness of things) as the fraudulent piece of timber lay its last hour on the ground, looking and smelling, to their guilty imaginations, like anything but ironbark, they were aware of the government inspector drifting down upon them obliquely, with something of the atmosphere of a casual Bill or Jim who had dropped out of his easygoing track to see how they were getting on, and borrow a match. They had more than half hoped that, as he had visited them pretty frequently during the progress of the work, and knew how near it was to completion, he wouldn't bother coming any more. But it's the way with the government. You might move heaven and earth in vain endeavour to get the "guvermunt" to flutter an eyelash over something of the most momentous importance to yourself and mates and the district—even to the country; but just when you are leaving authority severely alone, and have strong reasons for not wanting to worry or interrupt it, and not desiring it to worry about you, it will take a fancy into its head to come along and bother.

"It's always the way!" muttered Dave to his mates. "I knew the beggar would turn up! . . . And the only cronk log we've had, too!" he added, in an injured tone. "If this had 'a' been the only blessed ironbark in the whole contract, it would have been all right. . . . Good day, sir!" (to the inspector). "It's hot?"

The inspector nodded. He was not of an impulsive nature. He got down from his horse and looked at the girder in an abstracted way; and presently there came into his eyes a dreamy, far-away, sad sort of expression, as if there had been a very sad and painful occurrence in his family, way back in the past, and that piece of timber in some way reminded him of it and brought the old sorrow home to him. He blinked three times, and asked, in a subdued tone:

"Is that ironbark?"

Jack Bently, the fluent liar of the party, caught his breath with a jerk and coughed, to cover the gasp and gain time. "I—ironbark? Of course it is! I thought you would know ironbark, mister." (Mister was silent.) "What else d'yer think it is?"

The dreamy, abstracted expression was back. The inspector, by the way, didn't know much about timber, but he had a great deal of instinct, and went by it when in doubt.

"L—look here, mister!" put in Dave Regan, in a tone of innocent puzzlement and with a blank bucolic face. "B—but don't the plans and specifications say ironbark? Ours does, anyway. I—I'll git the papers from the tent and show yer, if yer like."

It was not necessary. The inspector admitted the fact slowly. He stooped, and with an absent air picked up a chip. He looked at it abstractedly for a moment, blinked his threefold blink; then, seeming to recollect an appointment, he woke up suddenly and asked briskly:

"Did this chip come off that girder?"

Blank silence. The inspector blinked six times, divided in threes, rapidly, mounted his horse, said "Day," and rode off.

Regan and party stared at each other.

"Wha—what did he do that for?" asked Andy Page, the third in the party.

"Do what for, you fool?" inquired Dave.

"Ta—take that chip for?"

"He's taking it to the office!" snarled Jack Bently.

"What—what for? What does he want to do that for?"

"To get it blanky well analysed! You ass! Now are yer satisfied?" And Jack sat down hard on the timber, jerked out his pipe, and said to Dave, in a sharp, toothache tone:

"Gimmiamatch!"

"We—well! what are we to do now?" inquired Andy, who was the hardest grafter, but altogether helpless, hopeless, and useless in a crisis like this.

"Grain and varnish the bloomin' culvert!" snapped Bently.

But Dave's eyes, that had been ruefully following the inspector, suddenly dilated. The inspector had ridden a short distance along the line, dismounted, thrown the bridle over a post, laid the chip (which was too big to go in his pocket) on top of it, got through the fence, and was now walking back at an angle across the line in the direction of the fencing party, who had worked up on the other side, a little more than opposite the culvert.

Dave took in the lay of the country at a glance and thought rapidly.

"Gimme an ironbark chip!" he said suddenly.

Bently, who was quick-witted when the track was shown him, as is a kangaroo-dog (Jack ran by sight, not scent), glanced in the line of Dave's eyes, jumped up, and got a chip about the same size as that which the inspector had taken.

Now the "lay of the country" sloped generally to the line from

Splitters

both sides, and the angle between the inspector's horse, the fencing party, and the culvert was well within a clear concave space; but a couple of hundred yards back from the line and parallel to it (on the side on which Dave's party worked their timber) a fringe of scrub ran to within a few yards of a point which would be about in line with a single tree on the cleared slope, the horse, and the fencing party.

Dave took the ironbark chip, ran along the bed of the water-course into the scrub, raced up the sidling behind the bushes, got safely through without breathing, across the exposed space, and brought the tree into line between him and the inspector, who was talking to the fencers. Then he began to work quickly down the slope towards the tree (which was a thin one), keeping it in line, his arms close to his sides, and working, as it were, down the trunk of the tree, as if the fencing party were kangaroos and Dave was trying to get a shot at them. The inspector, by the by, had a habit of glancing now and then in the direction of his horse, as though under the impression that it was flighty and restless and inclined to bolt on opportunity. It was an anxious moment for all parties concerned—except the inspector. They didn't want *him* to be perturbed. And, just as Dave reached the foot of the tree, the inspector finished what he had to say to the fencers, turned, and started to walk briskly back to his horse. There was a thunderstorm coming. Now was the critical moment—there were certain prearranged signals between Dave's party and the fencers which might have interested the inspector, but none to meet a case like this.

Jack Bently gasped, and started forward with an idea of intercepting the inspector and holding him for a few minutes in bogus conversation. Inspirations come to one at a critical moment, and it flashed on Jack's mind to send Andy instead. Andy looked as innocent and guileless as he was, but was uncomfortable in the vicinity of "funny business", and must have an honest excuse. "Not that that mattered," commented Jack afterwards; "it would have taken the inspector ten minutes to get at what Andy was driving at, whatever it was."

"Run, Andy! Tell him there's a heavy thunderstorm coming and he'd better stay in our humpy till it's over. Run! Don't stand staring like a blanky fool. He'll be gone!"

Andy started. But just then, as luck would have it, one of the fencers started after the inspector, hailing him as "Hi mister!" He wanted to be set right about the survey or something—or to pretend to want to be set right—from motives of policy which I haven't time to explain here.

That fencer explained afterwards to Dave's party that he "seen what you coves was up to", and that's why he called the inspector back. But he told them that after they had told their yarn—which was a mistake.

"Come back, Andy!" cried Jack Bently.

Dave Regan slipped round the tree, down on his hands and knees, and made quick time through the grass, which, luckily, grew pretty tall on the thirty or forty yards of slope between the tree and the horse. Close to the horse, a thought struck Dave that pulled him up, and sent a shiver along his spine and a hungry feeling under it. The horse would break away and bolt! But the case was desperate. Dave ventured an interrogatory "Cope, cope, cope?" The horse turned its head wearily and regarded him with a mild eye, as if he'd expected him to come, and come on all fours, and wondered what had kept him so long; then he went on thinking. Dave reached the foot of the post; the horse obligingly leaning over on the other leg. Dave reared head and shoulders cautiously behind the post, like a snake; his hand went up twice, swiftly—the first time he grabbed the inspector's chip, and the second time he put the ironbark one in its place. He drew down and back, and scuttled off for the tree like a gigantic tailless goanna.

A few minutes later he walked up to the culvert from along the creek, smoking hard to settle his nerves.

The sky seemed to darken suddenly; the first great drops of the thunderstorm came pelting down. The inspector hurried to his horse, and cantered off along the line in the direction of the fettlers' camp.

He had forgotten all about the chip, and left it on top of the post!

Dave Regan sat down on the beam in the rain and swore comprehensively.

The Buckjumper

SATURDAY afternoon.

There were about a dozen bush natives, from anywhere, most of them lanky and easygoing, hanging about the little slab-and-bark hotel on the edge of the scrub at Capertee Camp (a teamster's camp) when Cobb & Co's mailcoach and six came dashing down the sidling from round Crown Ridge, in all its glory, to the end of the twelve-mile stage. Some dusty, wiry, ill-used hacks were hanging to the fence and to saplings about the place. The fresh coach-horses stood ready in a stockyard close to the shanty. As the coach climbed the nearer bank of the creek at the foot of the ridge, six of the bushmen detached themselves from veranda-posts, from their heels, from the clay floor of the veranda and the rough slab wall against which they'd been resting, and joined a group of four or five who stood round one. He stood with his back to the corner post of the stockyard, his feet well braced out in front of him, and contemplated the toes of his tight new 'lastic-side boots and whistled softly. He was a clean-limbed, handsome fellow, with riding-cords, leggings, and a blue sash; he was Graeco-Roman-nosed, blue-eyed, and his glossy, curly black hair bunched up in front of the brim of a new cabbage-tree hat, set well back on his head.

"Do it for a quid, Jack?" asked one.

"Damned if I will, Jim!" said the young man at the post. "I'll do it for a fiver—not a blanky sprat less."

Jim took off his hat and shoved it round, and bobs were chucked into it. The result was about thirty shillings.

Jack glanced contemptuously into the crown of the hat.

"Not me!" he said, showing some emotion for the first time. "D'yer think I'm going to risk me blanky neck for your blanky amusement for thirty blanky bob? I'll ride the blanky horse for a fiver, and I'll feel the blanky quids in my pocket before I get on."

Meanwhile the coach had dashed up to the door of the shanty. There were about twenty passengers aboard—inside, on the box-seat, on the tailboard, and hanging on to the roof—most of them Sydney men going up to the Mudgee races. They got down and

13

went inside with the driver for a drink, while the stablemen changed horses. The bushmen raised their voices a little and argued.

One of the passengers was a big, stout, hearty man—a good-hearted, sporting man and a racehorse owner, according to his brands. He had a round red face and a white cork hat. "What's those chaps got on outside?" he asked the publican.

"Oh, it's a bet they've got on about riding a horse," replied the publican. "The flash-looking chap with the sash is Flash Jack, the horse-breaker; and they reckon they've got the champion outlaw in the district out there—that chestnut horse in the yard."

The sporting man was interested at once, and went out and joined the bushmen.

"Well, chaps! what have you got on here?" he asked cheerily.

"Oh," said Jim carelessly, "it's only a bit of a bet about ridin' that blanky chestnut in the corner of the yard there." He indicated an ungroomed chestnut horse, fenced off by a couple of long sapling poles in a corner of the stockyard. "Flash Jack there—he reckons he's the champion horse-breaker round here—Flash Jack reckons he can take it out of that horse first try."

"What's up with the horse?" inquired the big, red-faced man. "It looks quiet enough. Why, I'd ride it myself."

"Would yer?" said Jim, who had hair that stood straight up, and an innocent, inquiring expression. "Looks quiet, does he? *You* ought to know more about horses than to go by the looks of 'em. He's quiet enough just now, when there's no one near him; but you should have been here an hour ago. That horse has killed two men and put another chap's shoulder out—besides breaking a cove's leg. It took six of us all the morning to run him in and get the saddle on him; and now Flash Jack wants to back out of it."

"Euraliar!" remarked Flash Jack cheerfully. "I said I'd ride that blanky horse out of the yard for a fiver. I ain't goin' to risk my blanky neck for nothing and only to amuse you blanks."

"He said he'd ride the horse inside the yard for a quid," said Jim.

"And get smashed against the rails!" said Flash Jack. "I would be a fool. I'd rather take my chance outside in the scrub—and it's rough country round here."

"Well, how much do you want?" asked the man in the mushroom hat.

"A fiver, I said," replied Jack indifferently. "And the blanky stuff in my pocket before I get on the blanky horse."

"Are you frightened of us running away without paying you?" inquired one of the passengers who had gathered round.

"I'm frightened of the horse bolting with me without me being paid," said Flash Jack. "I know that horse; he's got a mouth like iron. I might be at the bottom of the cliff on Crown Ridge road in twenty minutes with my head caved in, and then what chance for the quids?"

"You wouldn't want 'em then," suggested a passenger. "Or, say! —we'd leave the fiver with the publican to bury you."

Flash Jack ignored that passenger. He eyed his boots and softly whistled a tune.

"All right!" said the man in the cork hat, putting his hand in his pocket. "I'll start with a quid; stump up, you chaps."

The five pounds were got together.

"I'll lay a quid to half a quid he don't stick on ten minutes!" shouted Jim to his mates as soon as he saw that the event was to come off. The passengers also betted amongst themselves. Flash Jack, after putting the money in his breeches-pocket, let down the rails and led the horse into the middle of the yard.

"Quiet as an old cow!" snorted a passenger in disgust. "I believe it's a sell!"

"Wait a bit," said Jim to the passenger, "wait a bit and you'll see."

They waited and saw.

Flash Jack leisurely mounted the horse, rode slowly out of the yard, and trotted briskly round the corner of the shanty and into the scrub, which swallowed him more completely than the sea might have done.

Most of the other bushmen mounted their horses and followed Flash Jack to a clearing in the scrub, at a safe distance from the shanty; then they dismounted and hung on to saplings, or leaned against their horses, while they laughed.

At the hotel there was just time for another drink. The driver climbed to his seat and shouted, "All aboard!" in his usual tone. The passengers climbed to their places, thinking hard. A mile or so along the road the man with the cork hat remarked, with much truth:

"Those blanky bushmen have got too much time to think." The bushmen returned to the shanty as soon as the coach was out of sight, and proceeded to "knock down" the fiver.

Hungerford

ONE of the hungriest cleared roads in New South Wales runs to within a couple of miles of Hungerford, and stops there; then you strike through the scrub to the town. There is no distant prospect of Hungerford—you don't see the town till you are quite close to it, and then two or three whitewashed galvanized-iron roofs start out of the mulga.

They say that a past Ministry commenced to clear the road from Bourke, under the impression that Hungerford was an important place, and went on, with the blindness peculiar to governments, till they got to within two miles of the town. Then they ran short of rum and rations, and sent a man on to get them, and make inquiries. The member never came back, and two more were sent to find him—or Hungerford. Three days later the two returned in an exhausted condition, and submitted a motion of want-of-confidence, which was lost. Then the whole House went on and was lost also. Strange to relate, that Government was never missed.

However, we found Hungerford and camped there for a day. The town is right on the Queensland border, and an interprovincial rabbit-proof fence—with rabbits on both sides of it—runs across the main street.

This fence is a standing joke with Australian rabbits—about the only joke they have out there, except the memory of Pasteur and poison and inoculation. It is amusing to go a little way out of town, about sunset, and watch them crack Noah's Ark rabbit jokes about that fence, and burrow under and play leap-frog over it till they get tired. One old buck rabbit sat up and nearly laughed his ears off at a joke of his own about that fence. He laughed so much that he couldn't get away when I reached for him. I could hardly eat him for laughing. I never saw a rabbit laugh before; but I've seen a possum do it.

Hungerford consists of two houses and a humpy in New South Wales, and five houses in Queensland. Characteristically enough, both the pubs are in Queensland. We got a glass of sour yeast at one and paid sixpence for it—we had asked for English ale.

The post office is in New South Wales, and the police barracks in Banana-land. The police cannot do anything if there's a row going on across the street in New South Wales, except to send to Brisbane and have an extradition warrant applied for; and they don't do much if there's a row in Queensland. Most of the rows are across the border, where the pubs are.

At least, I believe that's how it is, though the man who told me might have been a liar. Another man said he was a liar, but then *he* might have been a liar himself—a third person said he was one. I heard that there was a fight over it, but the man who told me about the fight might not have been telling the truth.

One part of the town swears at Brisbane when things go wrong, and the other part curses Sydney.

The country looks as though a great ash-heap had been spread out there, and mulga scrub and firewood planted—and neglected. The country looks just as bad for a hundred miles round Hungerford, and beyond that it gets worse—a blasted, barren wilderness that doesn't even howl. If it howled it would be a relief.

I believe that Burke and Wills found Hungerford, and it's a pity they did; but if I ever stand by the graves of the men who first travelled through this country, when there were neither roads nor stations, nor tanks, nor bores, nor pubs, I'll take my hat off. There were brave men in the land in those days.

It is said that the explorers gave the district its name chiefly because of the hunger they found there, which has remained there ever since. I don't know where the ford comes in—there's nothing to ford, except in flood-time. Hungerthirst would have been better. The town is supposed to be situated on the banks of a river called the Paroo, but we saw no water there, except what passed for it in a tank. The goats and sheep and dogs and the rest of the population drink there. It is dangerous to take too much of that water in a raw state.

Except in flood-time you couldn't find the bed of the river without the aid of a spirit-level and a long straight-edge. There is a custom-house against the fence on the northern side. A pound of tea often costs six shillings on that side, and you can get a common lead pencil for fourpence at the rival store across the street in the mother province. Also, a small loaf of sour bread sells for a shilling at the humpy aforementioned. Only about sixty per cent of the sugar will melt.

We saw one of the storekeepers give a dead-beat swagman five shillings' worth of rations to take him on into Queensland. The storekeepers often do this, and put it down on the loss side of their books. I hope the recording angel listens, and puts it down on the right side of his book.

We camped on the Queensland side of the fence, and after tea had a yarn with an old man who was minding a mixed flock of goats and sheep; and we asked him whether he thought Queensland was better than New South Wales, or the other way about.

He scratched the back of his head, and thought a while, and hesitated like a stranger who is going to do you a favour at some personal inconvenience.

At last, with the bored air of a man who had gone through the same performance too often before, he stepped deliberately up to the fence and spat over it into New South Wales. After which he got leisurely through and spat back on Queensland.

"That's what *I* think of the blanky colonies!" he said.

He gave us time to become sufficiently impressed; then he said: "And if I was at the Victorian and South Australian border I'd do the same thing."

He let that soak into our minds, and added: "And the same with West Australia—and—and Tasmania." Then he went away.

The last would have been a long spit—and he forgot Maoriland.

We heard afterwards that his name was Clancy and he had that day been offered a job droving at "twenty-five shillings a week and find your own horse". Also find your own horse-feed and tobacco and soap and other luxuries at station prices. Moreover, if you lost your own horse you would have to find another, and if that died or went astray you would have to find a third—or forfeit your pay and return on foot. The boss drover agreed to provide flour and mutton—when such things were procurable.

Consequently, Clancy's unfavourable opinion of the colonies.

My mate and I sat down on our swags against the fence to talk things over. One of us was very deaf. Presently a black-tracker went past and looked at us, and returned to the pub. Then a trooper in Queensland uniform came along and asked us what the trouble was about, and where we came from and were going, and where we camped. We said we were discussing private business, and he explained that he thought it was a row, and came over to see. Then he left us, and later on we saw him sitting with the rest of the population on a bench under the hotel veranda. Next morning we rolled up our swags and left Hungerford to the north-west.

The Loaded Dog

Dave Regan, Jim Bently, and Andy Page were sinking a shaft at Stony Creek in search of a rich gold quartz reef which was supposed to exist in the vicinity. There is always a rich reef supposed to exist in the vicinity; the only questions are whether it is ten feet or hundreds beneath the surface, and in which direction. They had struck some pretty solid rock, also water which kept them bailing. They used the old-fashioned blasting-powder and time-fuse. They'd make a sausage or cartridge of blasting-powder in a skin of strong calico or canvas, the mouth sewn and bound round the end of the fuse; they'd dip the cartridge in melted tallow to make it watertight, get the drill-hole as dry as possible, drop in the cartridge with some dry dust, and wad and ram with stiff clay and broken brick. Then they'd light the fuse and get out of the hole and wait. The result was usually an ugly pot-hole in the bottom of the shaft and half a barrow-load of broken rock.

There was plenty of fish in the creek, fresh-water bream, cod, cat-fish, and tailers. The party were fond of fish, and Andy and Dave of fishing. Andy would fish for three hours at a stretch if encouraged by a nibble or a bite now and then—say once in twenty minutes. The butcher was always willing to give meat in exchange for fish when they caught more than they could eat; but now it was winter, and these fish wouldn't bite. However, the creek was low, just a chain of muddy waterholes, from the hole with a few bucketfuls in it to the sizeable pool with an average depth of six or seven feet, and they could get fish by bailing out the smaller holes or muddying up the water in the larger ones till the fish rose to the surface. There was the cat-fish, with spikes growing out of the sides of its head, and if you got pricked you'd know it, as Dave said. Andy took off his boots, tucked up his trousers, and went into a hole one day to stir up the mud with his feet, and he knew it. Dave scooped one out with his hand and got pricked, and he knew it too; his arm swelled, and the pain throbbed up into his shoulder, and down into his stomach, too, he said, like a toothache he had once, and kept him awake for two nights—only the tooth-ache pain had a "burred edge", Dave said.

Dave got an idea.

"Why not blow the fish up in the big waterhole with a cart-ridge?" he said. "I'll try it."

He thought the thing out and Andy Page worked it out. Andy usually put Dave's theories into practice if they were practicable, or bore the blame for the failure and the chaffing of his mates if they weren't.

He made a cartridge about three times the size of those they used in the rock. Jim Bently said it was big enough to blow the bottom out of the river. The inner skin was of stout calico; Andy stuck the end of a six-foot piece of fuse well down in the powder and bound the mouth of the bag firmly to it with whipcord. The idea was to sink the cartridge in the water with the open end of the fuse attached to a float on the surface, ready for lighting. Andy dipped the cartridge in melted bees-wax to make it watertight. "We'll have to leave it some time before we light it," said Dave, "to give the fish time to get over their scare when we put it in, and come nosing round again; so we'll want it well watertight."

Round the cartridge Andy, at Dave's suggestion, bound a strip of sail canvas—that they used for making water-bags—to increase the force of the explosion, and round that he pasted layers of stiff brown paper—on the plan of the sort of fireworks we called "gun-crackers". He let the paper dry in the sun, then he sewed a covering of two thicknesses of canvas over it, and bound the thing from end to end with stout fishing-line. Dave's schemes were elaborate, and he often worked his inventions out to nothing. The cartridge was rigid and solid enough now—a formidable bomb; but Andy and Dave wanted to be sure. Andy sewed on another layer of canvas, dipped the cartridge in melted tallow, twisted a length of fencing-wire round it as an afterthought, dipped it in tallow again, and stood it carefully against a tent-peg, where he'd know where to find it, and wound the fuse loosely round it. Then he went to the camp-fire to try some potatoes which were boiling in their jackets in a billy, and to see about frying some chops for dinner. Dave and Jim were at work in the claim that morning.

They had a big black young retriever dog—or rather an over-grown pup, a big, foolish, four-footed mate, who was always slob-bering round them and lashing their legs with his heavy tail that swung round like a stockwhip. Most of his head was usually a red, idiotic slobbering grin of appreciation of his own silliness. He seemed to take life, the world, his two-legged mates, and his own instinct as a huge joke. He'd retrieve anything; he carted back most of the camp rubbish that Andy threw away. They had a cat that died in hot weather, and Andy threw it a good distance away in the scrub; and early one morning the dog found the cat, after it had been dead a week or so, and carried it back to camp, and laid it just inside the tent-flaps, where it could best make its presence known when the mates should rise and begin to sniff suspiciously in the sickly smothering atmosphere of the summer sunrise. He used to retrieve them when they went in swimming; he'd jump in after them, and take their hands in his mouth, and try to swim out with them, and scratch their naked bodies with his paws. They loved him for his good-heartedness and his foolishness, but when they wished to enjoy a swim they had to tie him up in camp.

He watched Andy with great interest all the morning making the cartridge, and hindered him considerably, trying to help; but about noon he went off to the claim to see how Dave and Jim were getting on, and to come home to dinner with them. Andy saw them coming, and put a panful of mutton-chops on the fire. Andy was cook today; Dave and Jim stood with their backs to the fire, as bushmen do in all weathers, waiting till dinner should be ready. The retriever went nosing round after something he seemed to have missed.

Andy's brain still worked on the cartridge; his eye was caught by the glare of an empty kerosene-tin lying in the bushes, and it struck him that it wouldn't be a bad idea to sink the cartridge packed with clay, sand, or stones in the tin, to increase the force of the explosion. He may have been all out, from a scientific point of view, but the notion looked all right to him. Jim Bently, by the way, wasn't interested in their "damned silliness". Andy noticed an empty treacle-tin—the sort with the little tin neck or spout soldered on to the top for the convenience of pouring out the treacle—and it struck him that this would have made the best kind of cartridge-case: he would only have had to pour in the powder, stick the fuse in through the neck, and cork and seal it with beeswax. He was turning to suggest this to Dave, when Dave glanced over his shoulder to see how the chops were doing—and bolted.

He explained afterwards that he thought he heard the pan spluttering extra, and looked to see if the chops were burning. Jim Bently looked behind and bolted after Dave. Andy stood stock-still, staring after them.

"Run, Andy! Run!" they shouted back at him. "Run! Look behind you, you fool!" Andy turned slowly and looked, and there, close behind him, was the retriever with the cartridge in his mouth —wedged into his broadest and silliest grin. And that wasn't all. The dog had come round the fire to Andy, and the loose end of the fuse had trailed and waggled over the burning sticks into the blaze; Andy had slit and nicked the firing end of the fuse well, and now it was hissing and spitting properly.

Andy's legs started with a jolt; his legs started before his brain did, and he made after Dave and Jim. And the dog followed Andy.

Dave and Jim were good runners—Jim the best—for a short distance; Andy was slow and heavy, but he had the strength and the wind and could last. The dog capered round him, delighted as a dog could be to find his mates, as he thought, on for a frolic. Dave and Jim kept shouting back, "Don't foller us! Don't foller us, you coloured fool!" But Andy kept on, no matter how they dodged. They could never explain, any more than the dog, why they followed each other, but so they ran, Dave keeping in Jim's track in all its turnings, Andy after Dave, and the dog circling round Andy—the live fuse swishing in all directions and hissing and spluttering and stinking. Jim yelling to Dave not to follow him, Dave shouting to Andy to go in another direction—to "spread out", and Andy roaring at the dog to go home. Then Andy's brain began to work, stimulated by the crisis: he tried to get a running kick at the dog, but the dog dodged; he snatched up sticks and stones and threw them at the dog and ran on again. The retriever saw that he'd made a mistake about Andy, and left him and bounded after Dave. Dave, who had the presence of mind to think that the fuse's time wasn't up yet, made a dive and a grab for the dog, caught him by the tail, and as he swung round snatched the cartridge out of his mouth and flung it as far as he could; the dog immediately bounded after it and retrieved it. Dave roared and cursed at the dog, who, seeing that Dave was offended, left him and went after Jim, who was well ahead. Jim swung to a sapling and went up it like a native bear; it was a young sapling, and Jim couldn't safely get more than ten or twelve feet from the ground.

The dog laid the cartridge, as carefully as if it were a kitten, at the foot of the sapling, and capered and leaped and whooped joyously round under Jim. The big pup reckoned that this was part of the lark—he was all right now—it was Jim who was out for a spree. The fuse sounded as if it were going a mile a minute. Jim tried to climb higher and the sapling bent and cracked. Jim fell on his feet and ran. The dog swooped on the cartridge and followed. It all took but a very few moments. Jim ran to a digger's hole, about ten feet deep, and dropped down into it—landing on soft mud—and was safe. The dog grinned sardonically down on him, over the edge, for a moment, as if he thought it would be a good lark to drop the cartridge down on Jim.

"Go away, Tommy," said Jim feebly, "go away."

The dog bounded off after Dave, who was the only one in sight now; Andy had dropped behind a log, where he lay flat on his face, having suddenly remembered a picture of the Russo-Turkish war with a circle of Turks lying flat on their faces (as if they were ashamed) round a newly-arrived shell.

There was a small hotel or shanty on the creek, on the main road, not far from the claim. Dave was desperate, the time flew much faster in his stimulated imagination than it did in reality, so he made for the shanty. There were several casual bushmen on the veranda and in the bar; Dave rushed into the bar, banging the door to behind him. "My dog!" he gasped, in reply to the astonished stare of the publican, "the blanky retriever—he's got a live cartridge in his mouth——"

The retriever, finding the front door shut against him, had bounded round and in by the back way, and now stood smiling in the doorway leading from the passage, the cartridge still in his mouth and the fuse spluttering. They burst out of that bar; Tommy bounded first after one and then after another, for, being a young dog, he tried to make friends with everybody.

The bushmen ran round corners, and some shut themselves in the stable. There was a new weatherboard and corrugated-iron kitchen and wash-house on piles in the backyard, with some women washing clothes inside. Dave and the publican bundled in there and shut the door—the publican cursing Dave and calling him a crimson fool, in hurried tones, and wanting to know what the hell he came here for.

The retriever went in under the kitchen, amongst the piles, but,

23

luckily for those inside, there was a vicious yellow mongrel cattle-
dog sulking and nursing his nastiness under there—a sneaking,
fighting, thieving canine, whom neighbours had tried for years to
shoot or poison. Tommy saw his danger—he'd had experience
from this dog—and started out and across the yard, still sticking to
the cartridge. Half-way across the yard the yellow dog caught him
and nipped him. Tommy dropped the cartridge, gave one terrified
yell, and took to the bush. The yellow dog followed him to the
fence and then ran back to see what he had dropped. Nearly a
dozen other dogs came from round all the corners and under the
buildings—spidery, thievish, cold-blooded kangaroo-dogs, mongrel
sheep- and cattle-dogs, vicious black and yellow dogs—that slip
after you in the dark, nip your heels, and vanish without explain-
ing—and yapping, yelping small fry. They kept at a respectable
distance round the nasty yellow dog, for it was dangerous to go
near him when he thought he had found something which might
be good for a dog or cat. He sniffed at the cartridge twice, and
was just taking a third cautious sniff when—

It was very good blasting-powder—a new brand that Dave had
recently got up from Sydney; and the cartridge had been ex-
cellently well made. Andy was very patient and painstaking in all
he did, and nearly as handy as the average sailor with needles,
twine, canvas and rope.

Bushmen say that that kitchen jumped off its piles and on again.
When the smoke and dust cleared away, the remains of the nasty
yellow dog were lying against the paling fence of the yard looking
as if he had been kicked into a fire by a horse and afterwards
rolled in the dust under a barrow, and finally thrown against the
fence from a distance. Several saddle-horses, which had been "hang-
ing-up" round the veranda, were galloping wildly down the road
in clouds of dust, with broken bridle-reins flying; and from a
circle round the outskirts, from every point of the compass in
the scrub, came the yelping of dogs. Two of them went home, to
the place where they were born, thirty miles away, and reached it
the same night and stayed there; it was not till towards evening
that the rest came back cautiously to make inquiries. One was
trying to walk on two legs, and most of 'em looked more or less
singed; and a little, singed, stumpy-tailed dog, who had been in
the habit of hopping the back half of him along on one leg, had
reason to be glad that he'd saved up the other leg all those years,

for he needed it now. There was one old one-eyed cattle-dog round that shanty for years afterwards, who couldn't stand the smell of a gun being cleaned. He it was who had taken an interest, only second to that of the yellow dog, in the cartridge. Bushmen said that it was amusing to slip up on his blind side and stick a dirty ramrod under his nose: he wouldn't wait to bring his solitary eye to bear—he'd take to the bush and stay out all night.

For half an hour or so after the explosion there were several bushmen round behind the stable who crouched, doubled up, against the wall, or rolled gently on the dust, trying to laugh without shrieking. There were two white women in hysterics at the house, and a half-caste rushing aimlessly round with a dipper of cold water. The publican was holding his wife tight and begging her between her squawks, to "Hold up for my sake, Mary, or I'll lam the life out of ye!"

Dave decided to apologize later on, "when things had settled a bit", and went back to camp. And the dog that had done it all, Tommy, the great, idiotic mongrel retriever, came slobbering round Dave and lashing his legs with his tail, and trotted home after him, smiling his broadest, longest, and reddest smile of amiability, and apparently satisfied for one afternoon with the fun he'd had.

Andy chained the dog up securely, and cooked some more chops, while Dave went to help Jim out of the hole.

And most of this is why, for years afterwards, lanky, easygoing bushmen, riding lazily past Dave's camp, would cry, in a lazy drawl and with just a hint of the nasal twang:

" 'Ello, Da-a-ve! How's the fishin' getting on, Da-a-ve?"

The Golden Graveyard

MOTHER MIDDLETON was an awful woman, an "old hand" (transported convict) some said. The prefix "mother" in Australia mostly means "old hag", and is applied in that sense. In early boyhood we understood, from old diggers, that Mother Middleton—in common with most other "old hands"—had been sent out for "knocking a donkey off a hen-roost". We had never seen a donkey. She drank like a fish and swore like a trooper when the spirit moved her; she went on periodical sprees, and swore on most occasions. There was a fearsome yarn, which impressed us greatly as boys, to the effect that once, in her best (or worst) days, she had pulled a mounted policeman off his horse, and half-killed him with a heavy pick-handle, which she used for poking down clothes in her boiler. She said that he had insulted her.

She could still knock down a tree and cut a load of firewood with any bushman; she was square and muscular, with arms like a navvy's; she had often worked shifts, below and on top, with her husband, when he'd be putting down a prospecting shaft without a mate, as he often had to do—because of her, mainly. Old diggers said that it was lovely to see how she'd spin up a heavy greenhide bucket full of clay and tailings, and land and empty it with a twist of her wrist. Most men were afraid of her, and few diggers' wives were strong-minded enough to seek a second row with Mother Middleton. Her voice could be heard right across Golden Gully and Specimen Flat, whether raised in argument or in friendly greeting. She came to the old Pipeclay diggings with the "rough crowd" (mostly Irish), and when the old and new Pipeclays were worked out, she went with the rush to Gulgong (about the last of the great alluvial or "poor-man's" goldfields) and came back to Pipeclay when the Log Paddock goldfield "broke out", adjacent to the old fields, and so helped prove the truth of the old diggers' saying, that no matter how thoroughly ground has been worked, there is always room for a new Ballarat.

Jimmy Middleton died at Log Paddock, and was buried, about

The newly arrived inquiring

The Newly Arrived Inquiring
Gift of Tony Hamilton and Miss S. E. Hamilton, 1967
Collection: City of Ballarat Fine Art Gallery

the last, in the little old cemetery—appertaining to the old farming town on the river, about four miles away—which adjoined the district racecourse, in the bush, on the far edge of Specimen Flat. She conducted the funeral. Some said she made the coffin, and there were alleged jokes to the effect that her tongue had provided the corpse; but this, I think, was unfair and cruel, for she loved Jimmy Middleton in her awful way, and was, for all I ever heard to the contrary, a good wife to him. She then lived in a hut in Log Paddock, on a little money in the bank, and did sewing and washing for single diggers.

I remember hearing her one morning in neighbourly conversation, carried on across the gully, with a selector, Peter Olsen, who was hopelessly slaving to farm a dusty patch in the scrub.

"Why don't you chuck up that dust-hole and go up-country and settle on good land, Peter Olsen? You're only slaving your stomach out here." (She didn't say stomach.)

Peter Olsen (mild-whiskered little man, afraid of his wife): "But then you know my wife is so delicate, Mrs Middleton. I wouldn't like to take her out in the bush."

Mrs Middleton: "Delicate be damned! She's only shamming!" (At her loudest.) "Why don't you kick her off the bed and the book out of her hand, and make her go to work? She's as delicate as I am. Are you a man, Peter Olsen, or a ——?"

This for the edification of the wife and of all within half a mile.

Log Paddock was "petering". There were a few claims still being worked down at the lowest end, where big red-and-white waste-heaps of clay and gravel, rising above the blue-grey gum-bushes, advertised deep sinking; and little, yellow, clay-stained streams, running towards the creek over the drought-parched surface, told of trouble with the water below—time lost in bailing and extra expense in timbering. And diggers came up with their flannels and moleskins yellow and heavy, and dripping with wet mullock.

Most of the diggers had gone to other fields, but there were a few prospecting, in parties and singly, out on the flats and amongst the ridges round Pipeclay. Sinking holes in search of a new Ballarat.

Dave Regan—lanky, easygoing bush native; Jim Bently—a bit of a "Flash Jack"; and Andy Page—a character like what Kit (in *The Old Curiosity Shop*) might have been after a voyage to Australia and some colonial experience. These three were mates from habit and not necessity, for it was all shallow sinking where they worked. They were poking down pot-holes in the scrub in the vicinity of the racecourse, where the sinking was from ten to fifteen feet.

Dave had theories—"ideers" or "notions" he called them; Jim Bently laid claim to none—he ran by sight, not scent, like a kangaroo-dog. Andy Page—by the way, great admirer and faithful retainer of Dave Regan—was simple and trusting but, on critical occasions, he was apt to be obstinately, uncomfortably, exasperatingly truthful, honest, and he had reverence for higher things.

Dave thought hard all one quiet drowsy Sunday afternoon, and next morning he, as head of the party, started to sink a hole as close to the cemetery fence as he dared. It was a nice quiet spot in the thick scrub, about three panels along the fence from the farthest corner post from the road. They bottomed here at nine feet, and found encouraging indications. They drove inwards at right angles to the fence, and at a point immediately beneath it they were "making tucker"; a few feet farther and they were making wages. The old alluvial bottom sloped gently that way. The bottom here, by the way, was shelving, brownish, rotten rock.

Just inside the cemetery fence, and at right angles to Dave's drive, lay the shell containing all that was left of the late fiercely lamented James Middleton, with older graves close at each end. A grave was supposed to be six feet deep, and local grave-diggers had been conscientious. The old alluvial bottom sloped from nine to fifteen feet here.

Dave worked the ground all round from the bottom of his shaft, timbering—i.e., putting in a sapling prop—here and there where he worked wide; but the "payable dirt" ran in under the cemetery, and in no other direction.

Dave, Jim, and Andy held a consultation in camp over their pipes after tea, as a result of which Andy next morning rolled up his swag, sorrowfully but firmly shook hands with Dave and Jim, and started to tramp outback to look for work on a sheep-station.

This was Dave's theory—drawn from a little experience and many long yarns with old diggers:—

He had bottomed on a slope to an old original watercourse, covered with clay and gravel from the hills by centuries of rains to the depth of from nine or ten to twenty feet; he had bottomed on a gutter running into the bed of the old buried creek, and carrying patches and streaks of wash (or gold-bearing dirt). If he went on he might strike it rich at any stroke of his pick; he might strike the rich lead which was supposed to exit round there. (There was always supposed to be a rich lead round there somewhere. "There's gold in them ridges yet—if a man can only git at it," says the toothless old relic of the Roaring Days.)

Dave might strike a ledge, pocket, or pot-hole holding wash rich with gold. He had prospected on the opposite side of the cemetery, found no gold, and the bottom sloping upwards towards the grave-yard. He had prospected at the back of the cemetery, found a few colours, and the bottom sloping downwards towards the point under the cemetery towards which all indications were now lead-ing him. He had sunk shafts across the road opposite the cemetery frontage and found the sinking twenty feet and not a colour of gold. Probably the whole of the ground under the cemetery was rich—maybe the richest in the district. The old grave-diggers had not been gold-diggers—besides, the graves, being six feet, would, none of them, have touched the alluvial bottom. There was nothing strange in the fact that none of the crowd of experienced diggers who rushed the district had thought of the cemetery and race-course. Old brick chimneys and houses, the clay for the bricks of which had been taken from sites of subsequent goldfields, had been put through the crushing-mill in subsequent years and had yielded payable gold. Fossicking Chinamen were said to have been the first to detect a case of this kind.

Dave reckoned to strike the lead (or a shelf or ledge with a good streak of wash lying along it) at a point about forty feet within the cemetery. But a theory in alluvial gold-mining was much like a theory in gambling, in some respects. The theory might be right enough, but old volcanic disturbances—"the shrinkage of the earth's surface", and that sort of old thing—upset everything. You might follow good gold along a ledge, just under the grass, till it suddenly broke off and the continuation might be a hundred feet or so under your nose.

Had the ground in the cemetery been "open" Dave would have gone to the point under which he expected the gold to lie, sunk a shaft there, and worked the ground. It would have been the quick-est and easiest way—it would have saved the labour and the time lost in dragging heavy buckets of dirt along a low lengthy drive to the shaft outside the fence. But it was very doubtful if the Government

29

could have been moved to open the cemetery even on the strong-est evidence of the existence of a rich goldfield under it, and backed by the influence of a number of diggers and their backers—which last was what Dave wished for at least of all. He wanted, above all things, to keep the thing shady. Then, again, the old clannish local spirit of the old farming town, rooted in years way back of the goldfields, would have been too strong for the Government, or even a rush of wild diggers.

"We'll work this thing on the strict Q.T.," said Dave.

He and Jim had a consultation by the camp-fire outside their tent. Jim grumbled, in conclusion:

"Well, then, best go under Jimmy Middleton. It's the shortest and straightest, and Jimmy's the freshest, anyway."

Then there was another trouble. How were they to account for the size of the waste-heap of clay on the surface which would be the result of such an extraordinary length of drive or tunnel for shallow sinkings? Dave had an idea of carrying some of the dirt away by night and putting it down a deserted shaft close by; but that would double the labour, and might lead to detection sooner than anything else. There were boys possum-hunting on those flats every night. Then Dave got an idea.

There was supposed to exist—and it has since been proved—another, a second gold-bearing alluvial bottom on that field, and several had tried for it. One, the town watchmaker, had sunk all his money in duffers, trying for the second bottom. It was supposed to exist at a depth of from eighty to a hundred feet—on solid rock, I suppose. This watchmaker, an Italian, would put men on to sink, and superintend in person, and whenever he came to a little colour-showing shelf, or false bottom, thirty or forty feet down—he'd go rooting round and spoil the shaft, and then start to sink another. It was extraordinary that he hadn't the sense to sink straight down, thoroughly test the second bottom, and if he found no gold there, to fill the shaft up to the other bottoms, or build platforms at the proper level and then explore them. He was living in a lunatic asylum the last time I heard of him. And the last time I heard from that field they were boring the ground like a sieve, with the latest machinery, to find the best place to put down a deep shaft, and finding gold from the second bottom on the bore. But I'm right off the line again.

"Old Pinter", Ballarat digger—his theory on second and other bottoms ran as follows:—

"Ye see *this* here grass surface—this here surface with trees an' grass on it, that we're livin' on, has got nothin' to do with us. This here bottom in the shaller sinkin's that we're workin' on is the slope to the bed of the *new* crick that was on the surface about the time that men was missin'-links. The false bottoms, thirty or forty feet down, kin be said to have been on the surface about the time that men was monkeys. The *secon'* bottom—eighty or a hundred feet down—was on the surface about the time when men was frogs. Now——"

But it's with the missing-link surface we have to do, and had the friends of the local departed known what Dave and Jim were up to they would have regarded them as something lower than missing-links.

"We'll give out we're tryin' for the second bottom," said Dave Regan. "We'll have to rig a fan for air, anyhow, and you don't want air in shallow sinkings."

"And someone will come poking round, and look down the hole and see the bottom," said Jim Bently.

"We must keep 'em away," said Dave. "Tar the bottom, or cover it with tarred canvas, to make it black. Then they won't see it. There's not many diggers left, and the rest are going; they're chucking up the claims in Log Paddock. Besides, I could get drunk and pick rows with the rest and they wouldn't come near me. The farmers ain't in love with us diggers, so they won't bother us. No man has a right to come poking round another man's claim: it ain't ettykit—I'll root up that old ettykit and stand to it—it's rather worn out now, but that's no matter. We'll shift the tent down near the claim and see that no one comes nosing round on Sunday. They'll think we're only some more second-bottom lunatics, like Francea [the mining watchmaker]. We're going to get our fortune out from under that old graveyard, Jim. You leave it all to me till you're born again with brains."

Dave's schemes were always elaborate, and that was why they so often came to the ground. He logged up his windlass platform a little higher, bent about eighty foot of rope to the bole of the windlass, which was a new one, and thereafter, whenever a suspicious-looking party (that is to say, a digger) hove in sight, Dave would let down about forty feet of rope and then wind, with simulated exertion, until the slack was taken up and the rope lifted the bucket from the shallow bottom.

"It would look better to have a whip-pole and a horse, but we can't afford them just yet," said Dave.

But I'm a little behind. They drove straight in under the cemetery, finding good wash all the way. The edge of Jimmy Middleton's box appeared in the top corner of the face (the working end) of the drive. They went under the butt-end of the grave. They shoved up the end of the shell with a prop, to prevent the possibility of an accident which might disturb the mound above; they puddled —i.e., rammed—stiff clay up round the edges to keep the loose earth from dribbling down; and having given the bottom of the coffin a good coat of tar, they got over, or rather under, an unpleasant matter.

Jim Bently smoked and burnt paper during his shift below, and grumbled a good deal. "Blowed if I ever thought I'd be rooting for gold down among the blanky dead men," he said. But the dirt panned out better every dish they washed, and Dave worked the wash out right and left as they drove.

But, one fine morning, who should come along but the very last man whom Dave wished to see round there—Old Pinter (James Poynton), Californian and Victorian digger of the old school. He'd been prospecting down the creek, carried his pick over his shoulder —threaded through the eye in the heft of his big-bladed, short-handled shovel that hung behind—and his gold-dish under his arm.

" 'Ello, Dave!" said Pinter, after looking with mild surprise at the size of Dave's waste-heap. "Tryin' for the second bottom?"

"Yes," said Dave, guttural.

Pinter dropped his tools with a clatter at the foot of the waste-heap and scratched under his ear like an old cockatoo, which bird he resembled. Then he went to the windlass, and resting his hands on his knees, he peered down, while Dave stood by helpless and hopeless.

Pinter straightened himself, blinking like an owl, and looked carelessly over the graveyard.

"Tryin' for a secon' bottom," he reflected absently. "Eh, Dave?"

Dave only stood and looked black.

Pinter tilted his head and scratched the roots of his chin-feathers, which stuck out all round like a dirty, ragged fan held horizontally.

"Kullers is safe," reflected Pinter.

"All right," snapped Dave. "I suppose we must let him into it."

"Kullers" was a big American buck nigger, and had been Pinter's mate for some time—Pinter was a man of odd mates; and what Pinter meant was that Kullers was safe to hold his tongue.

Next morning Pinter and his coloured mate appeared on the ground early, Pinter with some tools and the nigger with a wind-lass-bole on his shoulders. Pinter chose a spot about three panels or thirty feet along the other fence, the back fence of the cemetery, and started his hole. He lost no time for the sake of appearances; he sank his shaft and started to drive straight for the point under the cemetery for which Dave was making; he gave out that he had bottomed on good "indications" running in the other direction, and would work the ground outside the fence. Meanwhile Dave rigged a fan—partly for the sake of appearances, but mainly because his and Jim's lively imaginations made the air in the drive worse than it really was.

Dave was working the ground on each side as he went, when one morning a thought struck him that should have struck him the day Pinter went to work. He felt mad that it hadn't struck him sooner.

Pinter and Kullers had also shifted their tent down into a nice quiet place in the bush close handy; so, early next Sunday morning, while Pinter and Kullers were asleep, Dave posted Jim Bently to watch their tent, and whistle an alarm if they stirred, and then dropped down into Pinter's hole and saw at a glance what he was up to.

After that Dave lost no time: he drove straight on, encouraged by the thuds of Pinter's and Kullers's picks drawing nearer. They would strike his tunnel at right angles. Both parties worked long hours, only knocking off to fry a bit of steak in the pan, boil the billy, and throw themselves dressed on their bunks to get a few hours' sleep. Pinter had practical experience and a line clear of graves, and he made good time. The two parties now found it more comfortable to be not on speaking terms. Individually they grew furtive, and began to feel criminal like—at least Dave and Jim did. They'd start if a horse stumbled through the bush, and expected to see a mounted policeman ride up at any moment and hear him ask questions. They had driven about thirty-five feet when, one Saturday afternoon, the strain became too great, and Dave and Jim got drunk. The spree lasted over Sunday, and Monday morning they felt too shaky to come to work, and had more drink. On Monday afternoon, Kullers, whose shift it was below, stuck his pick through the face of his drive into the wall of Dave's, about four feet from the end of it: the clay flaked away, leaving a hole as big as a wash-hand basin. They knocked off for the day and decided to let the other party take the offensive.

Tuesday morning Dave and Jim came to work, still feeling shaky. Jim went below, crawled along the drive, lit his candle, and stuck it in the spiked iron socket and the spike in the wall of the drive, quite close to the hole, without noticing either the hole or the increased freshness of the air. He started picking away at the face and scraping the clay back from under his feet, and didn't hear Kullers come to work. Kullers came in softly and decided to try a bit of cheerful bluff. He stuck his great round black face through the hole, the whites of his eyes rolling horribly in the candle-light, and said, with a deep guffaw:

" 'Ullo! you dar'?"

No bandicoot ever went into his hole with the dogs after him quicker than Jim came out of his. He scrambled up the shaft by the foot-holes, and sat on the edge of the waste-heap, looking very pale.

"What's the matter?" asked Dave. "Have you seen a ghost?"

"I've seen the—the devil!" gasped Jim. "I'm—I'm done with this here ghoul business."

The parties got on speaking terms again. Dave was very warm, but Jim's language was worse. Pinter scratched his chin-feathers reflectively till the other party cooled. There was no appealing to the commissioner for goldfields; they were outside all law, whether of the goldfields or otherwise—so they did the only thing possible and sensible, they joined forces and became Poynton, Regan & Party. They agreed to work the ground from the separate shafts, and decided to go ahead, irrespective of appearances, and get as much dirt out and cradled as possible before the inevitable exposure came along. They found plenty of payable dirt, and soon the drive ended in a cluster of roomy chambers. They timbered up many coffins of various ages, burnt tarred canvas and brown paper, and kept the fan going. Outside they paid the storekeeper with difficulty and talked of hard times.

But one fine sunny morning, after about a week of partnership, they got a bad scare. Jim and Kullers were below, getting out dirt for all they were worth, and Pinter and Dave at their windlasses, when who should march down from the cemetery gate but Mother Middleton herself. She was a hard woman to look at. She still wore the old-fashioned crinoline and her hair in a greasy net; and on this as on most other sober occasions, she wore the expression of a rough Irish navvy who has just enough drink to make him nasty, and is looking out for an excuse for a row. She had a stride like a grenadier. A digger had once measured her step by her footprints in the mud where she had stepped across a gutter; it measured three feet from toe to heel.

She marched to the grave of Jimmy Middleton, laid a dingy bunch of flowers thereon, with the gesture of an angry man banging his fist down on the table, turned on her heel, and marched out. The diggers were dirt beneath her feet. Presently they heard her drive on in her spring-cart on her way into town, and they drew breaths of relief.

It was afternoon. Dave and Pinter were feeling tired, and were just deciding to knock off work for that day when they heard a scuffling in the direction of the different shafts, and both Jim and Kullers dropped down and bundled in in a great hurry. Jim chuckled in a silly way, as if there was something funny, and Kullers guffawed in sympathy.

"What's up now?" demanded Dave apprehensively.

"Mother Middleton," said Jim; "she's blind mad drunk, and she's got a bottle in one hand and a new pitchfork in the other, that she's bringing out for someone."

"How the hell did she drop to it?" exclaimed Pinter.

"Dunno," said Jim. "Anyway, she's coming for us. Listen to her!"

They didn't have to listen hard. The language which came down the shaft—they weren't sure which one—and along the drive was enough to scare up the dead and make them take to the bush.

"Why didn't you fools make off into the bush and give us a chance, instead of giving her a lead here?" asked Dave.

Jim and Kullers began to wish they had done so.

Mrs Middleton began to throw stones down the shaft—it was Pinter's—and they, even the oldest and most anxious, began to grin in spite of themselves, for they knew she couldn't hurt them from the surface, and that, though she had been a working digger herself, she couldn't fill both shafts before the fumes of liquor overtook her.

35

"I wonder which shaf' she'll come down?" asked Kullers in a tone befitting the place and occasion.

"You'd better go and watch your shaft, Pinter," said Dave, "and Jim and I'll watch mine."

"I—I won't," said Pinter hurriedly, "I'm—I'm a modest man."

Then they heard a clang in the direction of Pinter's shaft.

"She's thrown her bottle down," said Dave.

Jim crawled along the drive a piece, urged by curiosity, and returned hurriedly.

"She's broke the pitchfork off short, to use in the drive, and I believe she's coming down."

"Her crinoline'll handicap her," said Pinter vacantly, "that's a comfort."

"She's took it off!" said Dave excitedly; and peering along Pinter's drive, they saw first an elastic-sided boot, then a red-striped stocking, then a section of scarlet petticoat.

"Lemme out!" roared Pinter, lurching forward and making a swimming motion with his hands in the direction of Dave's drive. Kullers was already gone and Jim well on the way. Dave, lanky and awkward, scrambled up the shaft last. Mrs Middleton made good time, considering she had the darkness to face and didn't know the workings, and when Dave reached the top he had a tear in the leg of his moleskins, and the blood ran from a nasty scratch. But he didn't wait to argue over the price of a new pair of trousers. He made off through the bush in the direction of an encouraging whistle thrown back by Jim.

"She's too drunk to get her story listened to tonight," said Dave. "But tomorrow she'll bring the neighbourhood down on us."

"And she's enough, without the neighbourhood," reflected Pinter.

Some time after dark they returned cautiously, reconnoitred their camp, and after hiding in a hollow log such things as they couldn't carry, they rolled up their tents like the Arabs, and silently stole away.

A Vision of Sandy-blight

I'D been humping my back, and crouching and groaning for an hour or so in the darkest corner of the travellers' hut, tortured by the demon of sandy-blight. It was too hot to travel, and there was no one there except ourselves and Mitchell's cattle-pup. We were waiting till after sundown, for I couldn't have travelled in the daylight, anyway. Mitchell had tied a wet towel round my eyes, and led me for the last mile or two by another towel—one end fastened to his belt behind, and the other in my hand as I walked in his tracks. And oh! but this was a relief! It was out of the dust and glare, and the flies didn't come into the dark hut, and I could hump and stick my knees in my eyes and groan in comfort. I didn't want a thousand a year, or anything; I only wanted relief for my eyes— that was all I prayed for in this world. When the sun got down a bit, Mitchell started poking round, and presently he found amongst the rubbish a dirty-looking medicine bottle, corked tight; when he rubbed the dirt off a piece of notepaper that was pasted on, he saw "eye-water" written on it. He drew the cork with his teeth, smelt the water, stuck his little finger in, turned the bottle upside down, tasted the top of his finger, and reckoned the stuff was all right.

"Here! Wake up, Joe!" he shouted. "Here's a bottle of tears."

"A bottler wot?" I groaned.

"Eye-water," said Mitchell.

"Are you sure it's all right?" I didn't want to be poisoned or have my eyes burnt out by mistake; perhaps some burning acid had got into that bottle, or the label had been put on, or left on, in mistake or carelessness.

"I dunno," said Mitchell, "but there's no harm in tryin'."

I chanced it. I lay down on my back in a bunk, and Mitchell dragged my lids up and spilt half a bottle of eye-water over my eyeballs.

The relief was almost instantaneous. I never experienced such a quick cure in my life. I carried the bottle in my swag for a long time afterwards, with an idea of getting it analysed, but left it behind at last in a camp.

Mitchell scratched his head thoughtfully, and watched me for a while.

"I think I'll wait a bit longer," he said at last, "and if it doesn't blind you I'll put some in my eyes. I'm getting a touch of blight myself now. That's the fault of travelling with a mate who's always catching something that's no good to him."

As it grew dark outside we talked of sandy-blight and fly-bite, and sandflies up north, and ordinary flies, and branched off to Barcoo rot, and struck the track again at bees and bee stings. When we got to bees, Mitchell sat smoking for a while and looking dreamily backwards along tracks and branch tracks, and round corners and circles he had travelled, right back to the short, narrow, innocent bit of track that ends in a vague, misty point—like the end of a long, straight, cleared road in the moonlight—as far back. as we can remember.

"I had about fourteen hives," said Mitchell—"we used to call them 'swarms', no matter whether they were flying or in the box—when I left home first time. I kept them behind the shed, in the shade, on tables of galvanized-iron cases turned down on stakes; but I had to make legs later on, and stand them in pans of water, on account of the ants. When the bees swarmed—and some hives sent out the Lord knows how many swarms in a year, it seemed to me—we'd tin-kettle 'em, and throw water on 'em, to make 'em believe the biggest thunderstorm was coming to drown the oldest inhabitant; and, if they didn't get the start of us and rise, they'd settle on a branch—generally on one of the scraggy fruit-trees. It was rough on the bees—come to think of it; their instinct told them it was going to be fine, and the noise and water told them it was raining. They must have thought that nature was mad, drunk, or gone ratty, or the end of the world had come. We'd rig up a table, with a box upside down, under the branch, cover our face with a piece of mosquito-net, have rags burning round, and then give the branch a sudden jerk, turn the box down, and run. If we got most of the bees in, the rest that were hanging to the bough or flying round would follow, and then we reckoned we'd shook the queen in. If the bees in the box came out and joined the others, we'd reckon we hadn't shook the queen in, and go for them again. When a hive was full of honey we'd turn the box upside down, turn the empty box mouth down on top of it, and drum and hammer on the lower box with a stick till all the bees went up into the top box. I suppose it made their heads ache, and they went up on that account.

"I suppose things are done differently on proper bee-farms. I've heard that a bee-farmer will part a hanging swarm with his fingers, take out the queen bee and arrange matters with her; but our ways suited us, and there was a lot of expectation and running and excitement in it, especially when a swarm took us by surprise. The yell of 'Bees swarmin'!' was as good to us as the yell of 'Fight!' is now, or 'Bolt!' in town, or 'Fire!' or 'Man overboard!' at sea.

"There was tons of honey. The bees used to go to the vineyards at wine-making and get honey from the heaps of crushed grape-skins thrown out in the sun, and get so drunk sometimes that they wobbled in their bee-lines home. They'd fill all the boxes, and then build in between and under the bark, and board, and tin covers. They never seemed to get the idea out of their heads that this wasn't an evergreen country, and it wasn't going to snow all winter. My younger brother Joe used to put pieces of meat on the tables near the boxes, and in front of the holes where the bees went in and out, for the dogs to grab at. But one old dog, Black Bill, was a match for him; if it was worth Bill's while, he'd camp there, and keep Joe and the other dogs from touching the meat—once it was put down—till the bees turned in for the night. And Joe would get the other kids round there, and when they weren't looking or thinking, he'd brush the bees with a stick and run. I'd lam him when I caught him at it. He was an awful young devil, was Joe, and he grew up steady, and respectable, and respected—and I went to the bad. I never trust a good boy now. . . . Ah, well!

"I remember the first swarm we got. We'd been talking of getting a few swarms for a long time. That was what was the matter with us English and Irish and English-Irish Australian farmers: we used to talk so much about doing things while the Germans and Scotch did them. And we even talked in a lazy, easygoing sort of way.

"Well, one blazing hot day I saw father coming along the road, home to dinner (we had it in the middle of the day), with his axe over his shoulder. I noticed the axe particularly because father was bringing it home to grind, and Joe and I had to turn the stone; but when I noticed Joe dragging along home in the dust about fifty yards behind father I felt easier in my mind. Suddenly father dropped the axe and started to run back along the road towards Joe, who, as soon as he saw father coming, shied for the fence and got through. He thought he was going to catch it for something he'd done—or hadn't done. Joe used to do so many things and leave so many things not done that he could never be sure of father. Besides, father had a way of starting to hammer us unexpectedly—when the idea struck him. But father pulled himself up in about thirty yards and started to grab up handfuls of dust and sand and throw them into the air. My idea, in the first flash, was to get hold of the axe, for I thought it was sunstroke, and father might take it into his head to start chopping up the family before I could persuade him to put it (his head, I mean) in a bucket of water. But Joe came running like mad, yelling:

"'Swarmer—bees! Swawmmer—bee—ee—es! Bring—a—tin—dish—and—a—dippera—wa-a-ter!'

"I ran with a bucket of water and an old frying-pan, and pretty soon the rest of the family were on the spot, throwing dust and water, and banging everything, tin or iron, they could get hold of. The only bullock-bell in the district (if it was in the district) was on the old poley cow, and she'd been lost for a fortnight. Mother brought up the rear—but soon worked to the front—with a baking-dish and a big spoon. The old lady—she wasn't old then—had a deep-rooted prejudice that she could do everything better than anybody else, and that the selection and all on it would go to the dogs if she wasn't there to look after it. There was no jolting that idea out of her. She not only believed that she could do anything better than anybody, and hers was the only right or possible way, and that we'd do everything upside down if she wasn't there to do it or show us how—but she'd try to do things herself or insist on making us do them her way, and that led to messes and rows. She was excited now, and took command at once. She wasn't tongue-tied, and had no impediment in her speech.

"'Don't throw up the dust!—Stop throwing up dust!—Do you want to smother 'em?—Don't throw up so much water!—Only throw up a pannikin at a time!—D'yer want to drown 'em? Bang! Keep on banging, Joe!—Look at that child! Run, someone!—run! you, Jack!—D'yer want the child to be stung to death?—Take her inside . . . D'yer hear me? . . . Stop throwing up dust, Tom!' (to father). 'You're scaring 'em away! Can't you see they want to settle?' (Father was getting mad and yelping: 'For Godsake shettup and go inside.') 'Throw up water, Jack! Throw up—Tom! Take that bucket from him and don't make such a fool of yourself before the children! Throw up water! Throw—keep on banging, children! Keep on banging!' (Mother put her faith in banging.) 'There! —they're off! You've lost 'em! I knew you would! I told yer—keep on bang——!'

"A bee struck her in the eye, and she grabbed at it!

"Mother went home—and inside.

"Father was good at bees—could manage them like sheep when he got to know their ideas. When the swarm settled, he sent us for the old washing stool, boxes, bags, and so on; and the whole time he was fixing the bees I noticed that whenever his back was turned to us his shoulders would jerk up as if he was cold, and he seemed to shudder from inside, and now and then I'd hear a grunting sort of whimper like a boy that was just starting to blubber. But father wasn't weeping, and bees weren't stinging him; it was the bee that stung mother that was tickling father. When he went into the house, mother's other eye had bunged for sympathy. Father was always gentle and kind in sickness, and he bathed mother's eyes and rubbed mud on, but every now and then he'd catch inside, and jerk and shudder, and grunt and cough. Mother got wild, but presently the humour of it struck her, and she had to laugh, and a rum laugh it was, with both eyes bunged up. Then she got hysterical, and started to cry, and father put his arm round her shoulder and ordered us out of the house.

"They were very fond of each other, the old people were, under it all—right up to the end. . . . Ah, well!"

Mitchell pulled the swags out of a bunk, and started to fasten the nose-bags on.

Shooting the Moon

WE lay in camp in the fringe of the mulga, and watched the big, red, smoky, rising moon out on the edge of the misty plain, and smoked and thought together sociably. Our nose-bags were nice and heavy, and we still had about a pound of nailrod between us.

The moon reminded my mate, Jack Mitchell, of something—anything reminded him of something, in fact.

"Did you ever notice," said Jack, in a lazy tone, just as if he didn't want to tell a yarn—"Did you ever notice that people always shoot the moon when there's no moon? Have you got the matches?"

He lit up; he was always lighting up when he was reminded of something.

"This reminds me—Have you got the knife? My pipe's stuffed up."

He dug it out, loaded afresh, and lit up again.

"I remember once, at a pub I was staying at, I had to leave without saying good-bye to the landlord. I didn't know him very well at that time.

"My room was upstairs at the back, with the window opening on to the backyard. I always carried a bit of clothes-line in my swag or portmanteau those times. I travelled along with a portmanteau those times. I carried the rope in case of accident, or in case of fire, to lower my things out of the window—or hang myself, maybe, if things got too bad. No, now I come to think of it, I carried a revolver for that, and it was the only thing I never pawned."

"To hang yourself with?" asked the mate.

"Yes—you're very smart," snapped Mitchell; "never mind—— This reminds me that I got a chap at a pub to pawn my last suit, while I stopped inside and waited for an old mate to send me a pound; but I kept the shooter, and if he hadn't sent it I'd have been the late John Mitchell long ago."

"And sometimes you lower'd out when there wasn't a fire."

Night Camp

"Yes, that will pass; you're improving in the funny business. But about the yarn. There was two beds in my room at the pub, where I had to go away without shouting for the boss, and, as it happened, there was a strange chap sleeping in the other bed that night, and, just as I raised the window and was going to lower my bag out, he woke up.

" 'Now, look here,' I said, shaking my fist at him, like that, 'if you say a word, I'll stoush yer!'

" 'Well,' he said, 'well, you needn't be in such a sweat to jump down a man's throat. I've got my swag under the bed, and I was just going to ask you for the loan of the rope when you're done with it.'

"Well, we chummed. His name was Tom—Tom—something, I forget the other name, but it doesn't matter. Have you got the matches?"

He wasted three matches, and continued:

"There was a lot of old galvanized iron lying about under the window, and I was frightened the swag would make a noise; anyway, I'd have to drop the rope, and that was sure to make a noise. So we agreed for one of us to go down and land the swag. If we were seen going down without the swags it didn't matter, for we could say we wanted to go out in the yard for something."

"If you had the swag you might pretend you were walking in your sleep," I suggested, for want of something funnier to say.

"Bosh!" said Jack, "and get woke up with a black eye! Bushies don't generally carry their swags out of pubs in their sleep, or walk neither; it's only city swells who do that. Where's the blessed matches?

"Well, Tom agreed to go, and presently I saw a shadow under the window, and lowered away.

" 'All right?' I asked in a whisper.

" 'All right!' whispered the shadow.

"I lowered the other swag.

" 'All right?'

" 'All right!' said the shadow, and just then the moon came out.

" 'All right!' says the shadow.

"But it wasn't all right. It was the landlord himself!

"It seems he got up and went out to the back in the night, and just happened to be coming in when my mate Tom was sneaking out of the back door. He saw Tom, and Tom saw him, and smoked through a hole in the palings into the scrub. The boss looked up at the window, and dropped to it. I went down, funky enough, I can tell you, and faced him. He said:

" 'Look here, mate, why didn't you come straight to me, and tell me how you was fixed, instead of sneaking round the trouble in that fashion? There's no occasion for it.'

"I felt mean at once, but I said: 'Well, you see, we didn't know you, boss.'

" 'So it seems. Well, I didn't think of that. Anyway, call up your mate and come and have a drink; we'll talk over it afterwards.' So I called Tom. 'Come on,' I shouted. 'It's all right.'

"And the boss kept us a couple of days, and then gave us as much tucker as we could carry, and a drop of stuff and a few bob to go on the track again with."

"Well, he was white, any road."

"Yes, I knew him well after that, and only heard one man say a word against him."

"And did you stoush him?"

"No; I was going to, but Tom wouldn't let me. He said he was frightened I might make a mess of it, and he did it himself."

"Did what? Make a mess of it?"

"He made a mess of the other man that slandered that publican. I'd be funny if I was you. Where's the matches?"

"And could Tom fight?"

"Yes. Tom could fight."

"Did you travel long with him after that?"

"Ten years."

"And where is he now?"

"Dead—Give us the matches."

Bill, the Ventriloquial Rooster

"WHEN WE were up-country on the selection we had a rooster at our place named Bill," said Mitchell; "a big mongrel of no particular breed, though the old lady said he was a 'brammer'—and many an argument she had with the old man about it too; she was just as stubborn and obstinate in her opinion as the governor was in his. But, anyway, we called him Bill, and didn't take any particular notice of him till a cousin of some of us came from Sydney on a visit to the country, and stayed at our place because it was cheaper than stopping at a pub. Well, somehow this chap got interested in Bill, and studied him for two or three days, and at last he says:

" 'Why, that rooster's a ventriloquist!'

" 'A what?'

" 'A ventriloquist!'

" 'Go along with yer!'

" 'But he is. I've heard of cases like this before; but this is the first I've come across. Bill's a ventriloquist right enough.'

"Then we remembered that there wasn't another rooster within five miles—our only neighbour, an Irishman named Page, didn't have one at the time—and we'd often heard another cock crow, but didn't think to take any notice of it. We watched Bill, and sure enough he *was* a ventriloquist. The 'ka-cocka' would come all right, but the 'co-ka-koo-oi-oo' seemed to come from a distance. And sometimes the whole crow would go wrong, and come back like an echo that had been lost for a year. Bill would stand on tiptoe, and hold his elbows out, and curve his neck, and go two or three times as if he was swallowing nest-eggs, and nearly break his neck and burst his gizzard; and then there'd be no sound at all where he was—only a cock crowing in the distance.

"And pretty soon we could see that Bill was in great trouble about it himself. You see, he didn't know it was himself—thought it was another rooster challenging him, and he wanted badly to find that other bird. He would get up on the woodheap, and crow and listen—crow and listen again—crow and listen, and then he'd go up to the top of the paddock, and get up on the stack, and crow and listen there. Then down to the other end of the paddock, and get up on the mullock-heap, and crow and listen there. Then across to the other side and up on a log among the saplings, and crow 'n' listen some more. He searched all over the place for that other rooster, but of course couldn't find him. Sometimes he'd be out all day crowing and listening all over the country, and then come home dead tired, and rest and cool off in a hole that the hens had scratched for him in a damp place under the water-cask sledge.

"Well, one day Page brought home a big white rooster, and when he let it go it climbed up on Page's stack and crowed, to see if there was any more roosters round there. Bill had come home tired; it was a hot day, and he'd rooted out the hens, and was having a spell-oh under the cask when the white rooster crowed. Bill didn't lose any time getting out and on to the woodheap, and then he waited till he heard the crow again; then he crowed, and the other rooster crowed again, and they crowed at each other for three days, and called each other all the wretches they could lay their tongues to, and after that they implored each other to come out and be made into chicken soup and feather pillows. But neither'd come. You see, there were *three* crows—there was Bill's crow, and the ventriloquist crow, and the white rooster's crow—and each rooster thought that there was *two* roosters in the opposition camp, and that he mightn't get fair play, and, consequently, both were afraid to put up their hands.

"But at last Bill couldn't stand it any longer. He made up his mind to go and have it out, even if there was a whole agricultural show of prize and honourable-mention fighting-cocks in Page's yard. He got down from the woodheap and started off across the ploughed field, his head down, his elbows out, and his thick awkward legs prodding away at the furrows behind for all they were worth.

"I wanted to go down badly and see the fight, and barrack for Bill. But I daren't, because I'd been coming up the road late the night before with my brother Joe, and there was about three panels of turkeys roosting along on the top rail of Page's front fence; and we brushed 'em with a bough, and they got up such a blessed gobbling fuss about it that Page came out in his shirt and saw us running away; and I knew he was laying for us with a bullock-whip. Besides, there was friction between the two families on account of a thoroughbred bull that Page borrowed and wouldn't lend to us, and that got into our paddock on account of me mending a panel in the party fence, and carelessly leaving the top rail down after sundown while our cows was moving round there in the saplings.

"So there was too much friction for me to go down, but I climbed a tree as near the fence as I could and watched. Bill reckoned he'd found that rooster at last. The white rooster wouldn't come down from the stack, so Bill went up to him, and they fought there till they tumbled down the other side, and I couldn't see any more. Wasn't I wild? I'd have given my dog to have seen the rest of the fight. I went down to the far side of Page's fence and climbed a tree there, but of course I couldn't see anything, so I came home the back way. Just as I got home Page came round to the front and sung out, 'Insoid there!' And me and Jim went under the house like snakes and looked out round a pile. But Page was all right—he had a broad grin on his face, and Bill safe under his arm. He put Bill down on the ground very carefully, and says he to the old folks:

" 'Yer rooster knocked the stuffin' out of my rooster, but I bear no malice. 'Twas a grand foight.'

"And then the old man and Page had a yarn, and got pretty friendly after that. And Bill didn't seem to bother about any more ventriloquialism; but the white rooster spent a lot of time looking for that other rooster. Perhaps he thought he'd have better luck with him. But Page was on the look-out all the time to get a rooster that would lick ours. He did nothing else for a month but ride round and inquire about roosters; and at last he borrowed a game-bird in town, left five pounds deposit on him, and brought him home. And Page and the old man agreed to have a match—about the only thing they'd agreed about for five years. And they fixed it up for a Sunday when the old lady and the girls and kids were going on a visit to some relations, about fifteen miles away—to stop all night. The guv'nor made me go with them on horseback; but I knew what was up, and so my pony went lame about a mile along the road, and I had to come back and turn him out in the top paddock, and hide the saddle and bridle in a hollow log, and sneak home and climb up on the roof of the shed. It was an awful hot day, and I had to keep climbing backward and forward over the ridge-pole all the morning to keep out of sight of the old man, for he was moving about a good deal.

"Well, after dinner, the fellows from round about began to ride in and hang up their horses round the place till it looked as if there was going to be a funeral. Some of the chaps saw me, of course, but I tipped them the wink, and they gave me the office whenever the old man happened around.

"Well, Page came along with his game-rooster. Its name was Jim. It wasn't much to look at, and it seemed a good deal smaller and weaker than Bill. Some of the chaps were disgusted, and said it wasn't a game-rooster at all; Bill'd settle it in one lick, and they wouldn't have any fun.

"Well, they brought the game one out and put him down near the woodheap, and routed Bill out from under his cask. He got interested at once. He looked at Jim, and got up on the woodheap and crowed and looked at Jim again. He reckoned *this* at last was the fowl that had been humbugging him all along. Presently his trouble caught him, and then he'd crow and take a squint at the game 'un, and crow again, and have another squint at gamey, and try to crow and keep his eye on the game-rooster at the same time. But Jim never committed himself, until at last he happened to gape just after Bill's whole crow went wrong, and Bill spotted him. He reckoned he'd caught him this time, and he got down off that woodheap and went for the foe. But Jim ran away—and Bill ran after him.

"Round and round the woodheap they went, and round the shed, and round the house and under it, and back again, and round the woodheap and over it and round the other way, and kept it up for close on an hour. Bill's bill was just within an inch or so of the game-rooster's tail-feathers most of the time, but he couldn't get any nearer, do how he liked. And all the time the fellers kept chyackin' Page and singing out, 'What price your game un, Page! Go it, Bill! Go it, old cock!' and all that sort of thing. Well, the game rooster went as if it was a go-as-you-please, and he didn't care if it lasted a year. He didn't seem to take any interest in the business, but Bill got excited, and by and by he got mad. He held his head lower and lower and his wings further and further out from his sides, and prodded away harder and harder at the ground behind, but it wasn't any use. Jim seemed to keep ahead without trying. They stuck to the woodheap towards the last. They went round first one way for a while, and then the other for a change, and now and then they'd go over the top to break the monotony; and the chaps got more interested in the race than they would have been in the fight —and bet on it, too. But Bill was handicapped with his weight. He was done up at last; he slowed down till he couldn't waddle, and then, when he was thoroughly knocked up, that game-rooster turned on him, and gave him the father of a hiding.

"And my father caught me when I'd got down in the excitement, and wasn't thinking, and *he* gave *me* the stepfather of a hiding. But he had a lively time with the old lady afterwards, over the cock-fight.

"Bill was so disgusted with himself that he went under the cask and died."

Ah Dam

THE horse-ferry had its humorously exasperating side. The boats were high and flat and wouldn't steer. I have timed one to take three-quarters of an hour for the trip from Blue's Point to Dawes Point, a distance of a little less than half a mile. This included some half-dozen attempts to make land. When the steering gear or something went wrong, we'd have a trip round the harbour thrown in for our modest copper. The last time, I think, we went twice round the flagship; and the time before that I had a nice little run up the Parramatta River. I hadn't been there for years. On this occasion we came back on the other rudder, and went into dock wrong end first, with all the horses' heads turned back to Blue's Point. They had big meat and furniture vans and long timber trucks behind them and couldn't turn. So the ferry had to crawl back to Blue's Point, where the carts and vans and trucks were driven ashore and turned round somehow, and brought aboard again for another shot at it. I didn't mind it much, only a big German training-ship was lying at Blue's Point at the time, and officers and cadets could look down and smile on all this and on many other similar manœuvres going on daily in a very narrow waterway, between Australia's greatest city, and its nearest, wealthiest, and most fashionable front-garden suburb. That's what galled me. Similar accidents occur frequently on the passenger-ferries, but it doesn't seem to matter, and it won't till the big smash comes. And when that blows over, it will go on not mattering. Sydney people will stand anything. I remember the years when they wouldn't.

The horse-ferry levels all, from the latest expensive motor-car, with its load of veiled and tailored tolerant disgust, to the little turnout of Benno, the bottle-oh with *his* load of disgust, but untailored and intolerant; and so down to the derelict and the deadbeat, working their way over at the tail of a friendly cart, because they haven't the pennies to go through the turnstiles of the passenger-ferries. *Item:* The black, covered unobtrusive undertaker's cart, containing, in the cheapest of contract shells, the last vacated earthly

Sydney From Near St Leonards, North Shore

tenement—much damaged and dilapidated, no doubt—of some friendless outcast, or pauper dead.

But this is the chonicle of my acquaintance Ah Dam, a cousin (twice removed by law) of my friend Ah See, and the son of old Ah Soon, whose tale I have told before.

At least his name wasn't Ah Dam, but I could see he felt like it, and he sounded like it occasionally, while he was telling me the story, in spite of the humorously doleful smile, or grin, which is common in white, black, yellow, brown and brindle when they bump up against the Australian law. They don't grin much when they bump up against Chinese law—at least, not for long. Ah Dam told me that, and his father told him.

I might have to use Ah Dam again, so I will tell you a little about him. He's a Sydney-born Chinaman with a pigtail, and a merchant in a small way. His father, a native of Old China, made Ah Dam grow the pigtail, with the intention of taking the boy to China some day, and he gave Ah Dam a fairly good Chinese and English education. The old man went to China first, to smooth over old matters, perhaps, but he died there before he could send for Ah Dam and his mother. Whether the old 'un died of Chinese old age, or got mixed up in Chinese politics, or found that something that had happened in China in his youthful and pre-Australian days hadn't been forgotten, Ah Dam didn't tell me. Perhaps he didn't know. But in spite of its inconvenience, and the time and trouble it cost, and the derision it inspired in the bosom of dying-out larrikinism, Ah Dam stuck to the pigtail for the old man's sake.

And from what I know of Ah Dam, and in spite of his short-comings in one respect, I don't believe that the spirit of his old man has ever had cause to complain of any failure on the part of his Australian-born son to do the right thing by his father's memory. Though for the sake of convenience in census returns and in other documents, and for personal reasons, and business purposes occasionally, Ah Dam was supposed to be C.E. (Church of England), he told me, "Confucius".

His Chinese mother died—perhaps of a Chinese woman's broken Chinese heart—shortly after the news of the death of his father. And Ah Dam carried on the business, and prospered, and got the opium habit (his father and afterwards his mother had kept him carefully away from it—the manner of getting of the habit is another story), and he married a half-caste woman and had children.

I meant to say further back (but there isn't room for it now between the lines) that Ah Dam met his Port Arthur by way of the horse-ferry and Elder Man's Lane that leads up from it to George Street.

His opium "jag" was costing him 5s. a day, and 7s. 6d. a night. So he went aboard a boat from China, lying across the harbour, and manned by a Chinese crew. There had been preliminaries and arrangements, but this is making the story short. "There were fourteen of us," he said, with the aforesaid smile: but the rest were caught after he had got away. He blames himself for smoking that night. He should, on that occasion, of all occasions, have kept his senses unclouded. (How many of us have failed to do that same!) He seems to have got ashamed of his associates rather early—common Chinese forecastle coolies, and he a respectable and respected Sydney Chinese seed merchant, albeit in a small way. So he got one of the crew to row him ashore, unostentatiously (to avoid the bore and bother of farewell, perhaps), just about daylight, and land him in the scrubby, muddy, hulk-encumbered and nondescript little inlet between Neutral Bay and North Sydney. He should have gone round by Cammeray Park and loitered about in the safe vicinity of the Chinese gardens until a little more reasonable hour, and then have boldly walked up and taken the tram, like any decent vegetable or garden Chinaman going in on business or to consult his joss concerning the weather. But Ah Dam did none of these things. The spirit of the opium-cloud, in which he was enveloped, knew better than he did. Same as our drink fumes know better than we.

Perhaps Ah Dam shrank from a chance meeting with a Chinaman who knew him in the way of business, and might tell an acquaintance of his wife's or his friends, or his creditors (innocently enough perhaps) where he'd seen Ah Dam, and about what time of the day. Besides, opium-smoking was now an illegal offence, and severely punishable; and Ah Dam might have simply sought to cover up his immediate tracks for the sake of the fellow-smokers he had left behind on board, still smoking. Who can fathom the Oriental mind?

Anyway, Ah Dam went right round by devious ways to the horse-ferry—the first across, as it happened—where no decent

Chinaman was ever supposed to be without a cart or basket. He sat down and looked like nothing but a real Chinaman. There were two other alleged Chinamen aboard with carts and baskets, but they were not countrymen of his father's and they looked as bafflingly unconscious of his presence as he of anyone's. He gave up his ticket and strolled leisurely along Elder Man's Lane and into George Street, and down round the corner to the Seamen's Home, looking as bland and innocent and as mildly, tolerantly and benevolently interested in the world around him as seven Chinamen. Then he was aware, across the street on the opposite corner, of my other friend, Detective O'Kye, looking also as bland and innocent and as mildly, tolerantly and benevolently interested in the world around him as seventeen Chinamen. It was a critical moment. Ah Dam knew O'Kye, by sight (and also by sound and touch, for that matter), and the knowledge was mutual. And Ah Dam was as "dead cert." that O'Kye had noted him out of the corners of his innocent Irish eyes as O'Kye was that Ah Dam had spotted *him* out of the corners of *his* narrow, somewhat slanting, dark, reddish-brown Asiatic eyes.

They had met before twice. The last time was in Hobart, whither O'Kye has gone on some business with Ah Dam, who had pre-ceded him, but with no appointment whatever. They had drifted in sight of each other on opposite sides of the street—just as now— a few minutes after O'Kye had left the boat. And they had returned to Sydney together on the same boat, and had been very friendly and pleasant coming across. Ah Dam's society had fixed him up that time, and next Christmas he had sent O'Kye a present of a pair of the plumpest and tenderest young Muscovy ducks to be had. But all this in parentheses.

It was a critical moment, I say, but Ah Dam's mind was made up. He dived across the street with the action and manner of an impulsive English schoolboy on sighting an old chum (it sounds impossible for a Chinaman, but I have seen it done). He came up on the opposite kerb with a glad hand for O'Kye. (Ah Dam tells me all this himself.)

"How do, Mr O'Kye!" he cried. "You remember me? Hobart! Five years ago!"

"Why, it's Ah Dam!" said O'Kye, in pleased surprise; and he shook hands heartily. "How do you do, Ah Dam? Where have you been all this time? Still in the garden-seed business?"

"Yes, worse luck," said Ah Dam. "Same shop. Why you never come?"

"Oh, I'll drop in some day," said O'Kye. "How's the wife and kids? Quite well? How's business? You look quite like a man of leisure, Ah Dam. Taking a mornin' stroll before breakfast?"

"No damn fear!" said Ah Dam. "I was trying to catch a damn vegetable Chinaman from North Sydney. He owes me money. No use trying to catch him at home. He comes over 'bout this time, with his cart on Friday mornings, but I suppose he's gone by the long, Mr O'Kye. I must go back and open shop."

But O'Kye was not the man to let an old friend go like that, after not seeing him for years. He passed his arm through Ah Dam's in an affectionate, brotherly sort of way, and strolled back with him down George Street, and paused opposite a small place built in the Graeco-Roman-Moorish-Italian-Arabesque-Elizabethan-Egyptian-Chinese-Eskimo-American style of architecture, so much affected in Australia. He patted Ah Dam on the back and gently steered him in, as if he were going to treat his old friend to a good drink in a private bar, in defiance of Australian public or anti-Chinese opinion. It was No. 4 Police Station.

Ah Dam sighed a Chinese sigh, and handed over nine tins of opium from his inside coat pocket, and four from his pants—thirteen in all—and asked O'Kye to get him some Chinese tobacco. O'Kye nodded in a brotherly way, and went to get it, and Ah Dam retired to a cell.

I don't see any particular end or moral in this story, except, as Ah Dam put it to me himself: "You should always keep sober and your brains clear when you have any particular business on hand, and for some time before it."

The Spooks of Long Gully

THE first part of this sketch treats of a time when we were all "kids" together, and went two or three miles through Long Gully to the Old Bark School—whenever we couldn't get out of going—and took our dinners with us in our dinner-bags, and our home-lessons in our exercise books; and copied or corrected the said home-lessons from the model boy's book whenever we could get hold of it, or a squint at it by fraud, force, or bribery; when we thought it was "wicked" to swear, smoke, tell lies, or point at the moon—much to the disgust of the bad boy at school; when we regarded a shanty spree with childish horror; when we had a "conscience"; and when, nevertheless, we "wagged it" whenever the evil spirit moved us; and stole fruit, if it tempted us too much, and told "stories" to avoid a "hiding"—even as we do now to avoid starving—and teased the girls, and "went swimmin'" or "five-cornerin'" when we should have been studying; and when we believed in ghosts and fairies; and our principal ambitions were to be mounted troopers, bushrangers, and jockeys; when we were mostly true to each other, good Socialists without knowing it.

Long Gully was deep, dark, and deserted, and if it wasn't haunted, it should have been. It had the name of being haunted, anyway. One or two murders had certainly been committed there, to say nothing of others which had "been done right enough".

My earliest experience of the ghosts of Long Gully dates from a dim, uncertain Sunday evening, long years agone, when I was a youngster, or a "young 'un", or a "kid", as the local bushmen and hard-cases variously put it. I was returning home from a "five-cornerin'" expedition on the ridges in company with half a dozen schoolmates, and, somewhat to our dismay, darkness overtook us before we reached the end of the haunted gully. We were chased by the ghost of old Jack Drew. One of the other boys—it was Jim Bullock, I think—saw him first, close under the gap in Dead Man's Hollow, and, as near as I remember, he followed us right down to the foot of the gully. We ran. I didn't see the thing myself, but several others of the boys did—I took their word for it. Strictly speaking, we saw the ghost collectively rather than individually; and yet our several descriptions of the spook didn't agree—they differed in essential points. However, it was decided that the thing was the ghost of old Jack Drew, and none other, because it first appeared on the site of the hut where he had been found dead—with his throat cut, and a razor in his hand—years before.

Most of us agreed that it was a kind of shiny white thing, shaped like a man; and that the trees could be seen through it; and that it vanished from the middle of the road at the foot of the gully—seemed to fade away like. But Jim Bullock held out that the ghost was a sort of dead white, and didn't shine, and didn't vanish, but floated slowly up through the branches of the trees. I sided with him, because I didn't want to be behind, and because, with us, the minority, if Jim was in it, always seemed to hold respect in the end—anyway, it attracted the most attention, for the others would sink their differences and all join in an endeavour to "argue Jim out of it", which they couldn't.

An old bushman, who had known Drew in *his* time, was interviewed, and was of the opinion that the ghost went *down*; so the chances were that Jim Bullock was wrong. He stuck to his opinion, however, in spite of all opposition, and I stuck to him for the sake of the reflected light of his notoriety. He admitted one thing only, and that because he was sharp enough to see that it would add to his greatness; it was that the spook might have been sent after *him* as a "judgment" for his having unwittingly "pointed at the moon" on that same evening. Perhaps he felt a bit uneasy on that score, but he never let on; and after this the others regarded him with increased reverence, and "wot Jim Bullock said" carried greater weight than ever.

Another evening we were playing hide-and-seek about the deserted slab hut where old Grandfather Robinson died, and young Fred Dunn looked through a crack between two slabs and saw the ghost of old Robinson—or, at least, he said he saw it.

"Run! Run for your lives!" he yelled, taking the lead. "I seen old Robinson's ghost! It's inside! Come on away! Run for your lives!"

We ran—we ran hard, and didn't wait for air. The boy whose turn it was to hide, and for whom we'd been hunting unsuccessfully for the last half-hour, found himself without loss of time, and didn't lose any in catching up to us and trying to get home first.

Fred explained that he saw the ghost of the old man sitting at the table reading a newspaper. We objected, as soon as we recovered breath, to the effect that there was no table left in the hut; but Fred said that he never said there was a table; he seen the *ghost* of a table, and if we didn't believe him, let us go back and see—we might as well call him a liar.

At last we agreed to go back together, and Fred took the lead; but when we got to within a few yards of the hut someone declared that he saw something white gleaming through the cracks, and we came to a standstill, promptly and unanimously. Then Fred suddenly shouted: "There he is! He's coming out through the door! Look out! Here he comes!" and took to his heels.

We didn't wait to look. We ran for our natural lives, and took Fred's word for the rest.

I lately revisited the neighbourhood of Long Gully, and collected all the available information concerning the spooks. The following is the result of my labours:

Tom Quinn, a respectable and sober farmer, residing about a mile from the head of the gully, was returning home from town one night rather late, and he took the rough track through the gully by way of a short cut. He was driving up the steep "pinch" which led to the gap when he fancied he heard a peculiar noise behind—a "rum" noise he said it was. He looked round and saw the ghost of a woman following the cart. She was dressed in black, and had long, black hair, and had big, shining eyes, which last were fixed on him (and they made an impression, no doubt). She was gliding along behind the cart, with her hand laid on the top of the tail-board. Her face was a "sort er dull, dead white". He thought at first that she was a real woman, and wanted a lift, so he pulled up, but when he looked round again she was gone. Then he thought she was drunk, or "luny", and had got under the cart; so he drove on a piece, and looked round, but she'd vanished. Then he drove like mad for home. He jumped out of the cart, left it standing in the middle of the road in front of his house, and went in and laid down. He never said a word until the next morning. It was generally agreed, locally, that he had seen the ghost of a carrier's wife who had been murdered in the gully by her husband some fifteen years before.

I interviewed Jim Block, an old splitter, who had camped in the gully for a month or two. He couldn't say he seen anything, but he'd heerd some rum noises in the night. He wasn't frightened so long as he seed nothing, but he didn't like camping there. He heerd footsteps and things, and a noise like a man being knocked on the head. Ole Crow had camped in the same hut, and could tell me some rum things about it if he liked.

I saw "Ole Crow". He never heard nothing, but he saw some "rummy" things. Old Dean could tell me more about it than he could; but I'd better not ask Dean, for he didn't generally like to talk about it. An old cove named Grump had come home through the gully one night, and they say he was never the same afterwards. But old Grump was dead. I tried to pump Crow about the "rummy" things he "seed", but couldn't get any satisfaction out of him.

I next saw old Jarge Bullen, who'd lived in a hut under Dead Man's Gap. He never saw no ghosts, but he'd seen a " 'airy man". He'd been splitting, and was coming down the ridge after sundown when he heard a rum sort of noise, like a cart-horse coming down the sidling. He looked up and saw a big thing, like a giant covered with long red hair. It was "summat like a yourang ertang". Jarge ran, and the hairy man followed him "clean up to the hut". He had just time to get in and barricade the door. The hairy man went "snuffing and sniffing" round all night, scratching the bark and trying the door, and went away about daylight. Jarge shifted out of the gully next day, for he didn't want to spend a night like that again.

It was also reported that an old fossicker named "Corny George" had been chased in Long Gully by a hairy man and three ghosts. He arrived at a farm next morning in a fearfully excited condition, and died in the delirium tremens a few weeks later.

A young drover named Joe Phipps didn't see any ghost himself, but his brother Ted did. "Ted was comin' home one night from a dance, and was ridin' through Long Gully when his horse shied at somethin' near the road. Ted looked and saw a kind of white thing, like a woman standin' near the track; it glided across the road and disappeared into the scrub. Ted couldn't get his horse to move afterwards; it only stood stock-still and trembled. Ted had to take the saddle and bridle off and carry them home, leavin' the horse there. After that the same horse always jibbed at that same spot, and Joe often had to hump the saddle home himself. Lord strike him dead if he didn't! Ted didn't get over it for three days." He was at present on the Lachlan, so we didn't see him.

We also heard that an old Irishwoman, who lived on a small selection below the gully, had been visited by one of the spooks; but it turned out on investigation that it wasn't a ghost she saw. It was an angel. According to her account she was sitting alone in her kitchen one night reading the Bible when the "blessed" angel came to her and told her that her son, who lived ten miles away, was dying. The strangest part of it was that the son did die that night in the "horrors" in a shanty. The angel told the old woman that she wasn't to fret, for her son was going to a better world; that he would lose nothing by pegging out (or words in that direction), which was very true. The angel also said that his relations must bear up against the sorrow of his loss, and be resigned. They did, and also they were. So did the neighbours. The district could have lost several better men without much grief. The old woman was not sure about the identity of the spirit; it left no card. She thought it was either Gabriel or her departed husband, and was inclined to the latter part of her opinion. Local heathens insinuated that it was gin. She stated that her visitor was dressed in shining white and wore a pair of wings and a calm and holy and peaceful expression. Friends who had known her husband were of the opinion that it was Gabriel she saw.

Some school children had been chased by the spook of War Kee, a Chinaman who died there since my time. It would appear that some of the said school children had been in the habit of teasing War Kee when he was in the flesh, and consequently his reappearance as a ghost caused no small commotion amongst them. I interviewed one of them. He said he hadn't seen the spectre himself, but he heard it following behind. He was too frightened to look round. Young Jack Dunn (son of Fred, my old schoolmate) was a little behind the rest, and saw the ghost. Young Jack said that it kept singing out, "Give me back my pigtail! Give me back my pigtail!" But none of the others never heard it, 'cepting Jack's little brother Jimmy. Jimmy said that he was chased wonst by a big white thing with a flamin' red eye in the middle of its forehead an' a green eye in the back of its head; but I wasn't to take too much notice of that because young Jimmy was allers tellin' them sort of yarns. Besides, how could he see the green eye in the back of the ghost's head if he was chased?

The youngster evidently considered this a clincher; but young Jimmy came forward at this point and explained that the ghost ran both ways, "sometimes backids and sometimes forrids". But young Jack routed little Jimmy by asking him how he knew which was the front and which was the back of the spook in question.

I collected a great deal of evidence besides the above; but it is mostly unreliable, and so I refrain from publishing it.

One peculiarity about the ghosts of Long Gully, and one which I can't help noticing, is that they always "chase" people on sight, especially children, but never catch anybody. They must be very slow ghosts. It was, indeed, reported that one of them really did catch old Boozer Reid in the gully one night; but his account of the business was so disjointed and lurid, and so evidently over-drawn and exaggerated, that I could not, in justice to the more respectable spooks of Long Gully, believe him to the extent of publishing his evidence.

Bush Cats

"DOMESTIC CATS" we mean—the descendants of cats who came from the northern world during the last hundred-odd years. We do not know the name of the vessel in which the first Thomas and his Maria came out to Australia, but we suppose that it was one of the ships of the First Fleet. Most likely Maria had kittens on the voyage—two lots, perhaps—the majority of which were buried at sea; and no doubt the disembarkation caused her much maternal anxiety.

The feline race has not altered much in Australia, from a physical point of view—not yet. The rabbit has developed into something like a cross between a kangaroo and a possum, but the bush has not begun to develop the common cat. She is just as sedate and mother-ly as the mummy cats of Egypt were, but she takes longer strolls of nights, climbs gum-trees instead of roofs, and hunts stranger vermin than ever came under the observation of her northern an-cestors. Her views have widened. She is mostly thinner than the English farm cat—which is, they say, on account of eating lizards.

English rats and English mice—we say "English" because every-thing which isn't Australian in Australia *is* English (or British)—English rats and English mice are either rare or non-existent in the bush; but the hut cat has a wider range for game. She is always dragging in things which are unknown in the halls of zoology; ugly, loathsome, crawling abortions which have not been classified yet—and perhaps could not be.

The Australian zoologist ought to rake up some more dead lang-uages, and then go outback with a few bush cats.

The Australian bush cat has a nasty, unpleasant habit of drag-ging a long, wriggling, horrid black snake—she seems to prefer black snakes—into a room where there are ladies, proudly laying it down in a conspicuous place (usually in front of the exit), and then look-ing up for approbation. She wonders, perhaps, why the visitors are in such a hurry to leave.

Pussy doesn't approve of live snakes round the place, especially if she has kittens; and if she finds a snake in the vicinity of her progeny—well, it is bad for that particular serpent.

This brings recollections of a neighbour's cat who went out in the scrub, one midsummer's day, and found a brown snake. Her name—the cat's name—was Mary Ann. She got hold of the snake all right, just within an inch of its head; but it got the rest of its length wound round her body and squeezed about eight lives out of her. She had the presence of mind to keep her hold; but it struck her that she was in a fix, and that if she wanted to save her ninth life it wouldn't be a bad idea to go home for help. So she started home, snake and all.

The family were at dinner when Mary Ann came in, and, although she stood on an open part of the floor, no one noticed her for a while. She couldn't ask for help, for her mouth was too full of snake. By and by one of the girls glanced round, and then went over the table, with a shriek, and out of the back door. The room was cleared very quickly. The eldest boy got a long-handled shovel, and in another second would have killed more cat than snake; but his father interfered. The father was a shearer, and Mary Ann was a favourite cat with him. He got a pair of shears from the shelf and deftly shore off the snake's head, and one side of Mary Ann's whiskers. She didn't think it safe to let go yet. She kept her teeth in the neck until the selector snipped the rest of the snake off her. The bits were carried out on a shovel to die at sundown. Mary Ann had a good drink of milk and then got her tongue out and licked herself back into the proper shape for a cat; after which she went out to look for that snake's mate. She found it, too, and dragged it home the same evening.

Cats will kill rabbits and drag them home. We knew a fossicker whose cat used to bring him a bunny nearly every night. The fossicker had rabbits for breakfast until he got sick of them, and then he used to swap them with a butcher for meat. The cat was name Ingersoll, which indicates his sex and gives an inkling to his master's religious and political opinions. Ingersoll used to prospect round in the gloaming until he found some rabbit-holes which showed encouraging indications. He would shepherd one hole for an hour or so every evening until he found it was a duffer, or worked it out; then he would shift to another. One day he prospected a big hollow log with a lot of holes in it, and more going down underneath. The indications were very good, but Ingersoll had no luck. The game had too many ways of getting out and in. He found that he could not work that claim by himself, so he floated it into a company. He persuaded several cats from a neighbouring selection to take shares, and they watched the holes together, or in turns—they worked shifts. The dividends more than realized even their wildest expectations, for each cat took home at least one rabbit every night for a week.

A selector started a vegetable garden about the time when rabbits were beginning to get troublesome up-country. The hare had not shown itself yet. The farmer kept quite a regiment of cats to protect his garden—and they protected it. He would shut the cats up all day with nothing to eat, and let them out about sundown; then they would mooch off to the turnip patch like farm-labourers going to work. They would drag the rabbits home to the back door, and sit there and watch them until the farmer opened the door and served out the ration of milk. Then the cats would turn in. He nearly always found a semicircle of dead rabbits and watchful cats round the door in the morning. They sold the product of their labour direct to the farmer for milk. It didn't matter if one cat had been unlucky—had not got a rabbit—each had an equal share in the general result. They were true socialists, those cats.

One of those cats was a mighty big Tom, named Jack. He was death on rabbits; he would work hard all night, laying for them and dragging them home. Some weeks he would graft every night, and at other times every other night, but he was generally pretty regular. When he reckoned he had done an extra night's work he would take the next night off and go three miles to the nearest neighbour's to see his Maria and take her out for a stroll. Well, one evening Jack went into the garden and chose a place where there was good cover, and lay low. He was a bit earlier than usual, so he thought he would have a doze till rabbit time. By and by he heard a noise, and slowly, cautiously opening one eye, he saw two big ears sticking out of the leaves in front of him. He judged that it was an extra big bunny, so he put some extra style into his manœuvres. In about five minutes he made his spring. He must have thought (if cats think) that it was a whopping, old-man rabbit, for it was a pioneer hare—not an ordinary English hare, but one of those great coarse lanky things which the bush is breeding. The selector was attracted by an unusual commotion and a cloud of

63

dust among his cabbages, and came along with his gun in time to witness the fight. First Jack would drag the hare, and then the hare would drag Jack; sometimes they would be down together, and then Jack would use his hind claws with effect; finally he got his teeth in the right place, and triumphed. Then he started to drag the corpse home, but he had to give it best and ask his master to lend a hand. The selector took up the hare, and Jack followed home, much to the family's surprise. He did not go back to work that night; he took a spell. He had a drink of milk, licked the dust off himself, washed it down with another drink, and sat in front of the fire and thought for a goodish while. Then he got up, walked over to the corner where the hare was lying, had a good look at it, came back to the fire, sat down again, and thought hard. He was still thinking when the family retired.

A Droving Yarn

ANDY MACULLOCH had heard that old Bill Barker, the well-known overland drover, had died over on the Westralian side, and Dave Regan told a yarn about Bill.

"Bill Barker," said Dave, talking round his pipe stem, "was the *quintessence* of a drover——"

"The watter, Dave?" came the voice of Jim Bently, in startled tones, from the gloom on the far end of the veranda.

"The quintessence," said Dave, taking his pipe out of his mouth. "You shut up, Jim. As I said, Bill Barker was the quintessence of a drover. He'd been at the game ever since he was a nipper. He ran away from home when he was fourteen and went up into Queensland. He's been all over Queensland and New South Wales and most of South Australia, and a good deal of the Western, too: over the great stock-routes from one end to the other, Lord knows how many times. No man could keep up with him riding out, and no one could bring a mob of cattle or a flock of sheep through like him. He knew every trick of the game; if there was grass to be had Bill'd get it, no matter whose run it was on. One of his games in a dry season was to let his mob get boxed with the station stock on a run where there was grass, and before Bill's men and the station-hands could cut 'em out, the travelling stock would have a good bellyful to carry them on the track. Billy was the daddy of the drovers. Some said that he could ride in his sleep, and that he had one old horse that could jog along in his sleep, too, and that—travelling out from home to take charge of a mob of bullocks or a flock of sheep —Bill and his horse would often wake up at daylight and blink round to see where they were and how far they'd got. Then Bill would make a fire and boil his quart-pot, and roast a bit of mutton, while his horse had a mouthful of grass and a spell.

"You remember Bill, Andy? Big dark man, and a joker of the loud sort. Never slept with a blanket over him—always folded under him on the sand or grass. Seldom wore a coat on the route— though he always carried one with him, in case he came across a bush ball or a funeral. Moleskins, flannel waistcoat, cabbage-tree hat and 'lastic-side boots. When it was roasting hot on the plains and the men swore at the heat, Bill would yell, 'Call this hot? Why, you blanks, I'm freezin'! Where's me overcoat?' When it was raining and hailing and freezing on Bell's Line in the Blue Mountains in winter, and someone shivered and asked, 'Is it cold enough for yer now, Bill?' 'Cold!' Bill would bellow, 'I'm sweatin'!'

"I remember it well. I was little more than a youngster then—Bill Barker came past our place with about a thousand fat sheep for the Homebush sale-yards at Sydney, and he gave me a job to help him down with them on Bell's Line over the mountains, and mighty proud I was to go with him, I can tell you. One night we camped on the Cudgegong River. The country was dry and pretty close cropped and we'd been 'sweating' the paddocks all along there for our horses. You see, where there weren't sliprails handy we'd just take the tomahawk and nick the top of a straight-grained fence-post, just above the mortise, knock out the wood there, lift the top rail out and down, and jump the horses in over the lower one—it was all two-rail fences around there with sheep wires under the lower rail. And about daylight we'd have the horses out, lift back the rail, and fit in the chock that we'd knocked out. Simple as striking matches, wasn't it?

"Well, the horses were getting a good bellyful in the police horse paddock at night, and Bill took the first watch with the sheep. It was very cold and frosty on the flat and he thought the sheep might make back for the ridges, it's always warmer up in the ridges in winter out of the frost. Bill roused me out about midnight. 'There's the sheep,' he says, pointing to a white blur. 'They've settled down. I think they'll be quiet till daylight. Don't go round them; there's no occasion to go near 'em. You can stop by the fire and keep an eye on 'em.'

"The night seemed very long. I watched and smoked and toasted my shins, and warmed the billy now and then, and thought up pretty much the same sort of old things that fellers on night watch think over all over the world. Bill lay on his blanket, with his back to the fire and his arm under his head—freezing on one side and roasting on the other. He never moved—I itched once or twice to turn him over and bake the front of him—I reckoned he was about done behind.

"At last daylight showed. I took the billy and started down to the river to get some water to make coffee; but half-way down, near the sheep camp, I stopped and stared, I was never so surprised

Homeward Bound

in my life. The white blur of sheep had developed into a couple of acres of long dead silver grass!

"I woke Bill, and he swore as I never heard a man swear before —nor since. He swore at the sheep, and the grass, and at me; but it would have wasted time, and besides I was too sleepy and tired to fight. But we found those sheep scattered over a scrubby ridge about seven miles back, so they must have slipped away back of the grass and started early in Bill's watch, and Bill must have watched that blessed grass for the first half of the night and then set me to watch it. He couldn't get away from that.

"I wondered what the chaps would say if it got round that Bill Barker, the boss overland drover, had lost a thousand sheep in clear country with fences all round; and I suppose he thought that way too, for he kept me with him right down to Homebush, and when he paid me off he threw in an extra quid, and he said:

"'Now, listen here, Dave! If I ever hear a word from anyone about watching that gory grass, I'll find you, Dave, and murder you, if you're in wide Australia. I'll screw your neck, so look out.'

"But he's dead now, so it doesn't matter."

There was silence for some time after Dave had finished. The chaps made no comment on the yarn, either one way or the other, but sat smoking thoughtfully, and in a vague atmosphere as of sadness —as if they'd just heard of their mother's death and had not been listening to an allegedly humorous yarn.

Then the voice of old Peter, the station-hand, was heard to growl from the darkness at the end of the hut, where he sat on a three-bushel bag on the ground with his back to the slabs.

"What's old Peter growlin' about?" someone asked.

"He wants to know where Dave got that word," someone else replied.

"What word?"

"*Quint-essents.*"

There was a chuckle.

"He got it outback, Peter," said Mitchell, the shearer. "He got it from a newchum."

"How much did yer give for it, Dave?" growled Peter.

"Five shillings, Peter," said Dave, round his pipe stem. "And a stick of tobacco thrown in."

Peter seemed satisfied, for he was heard no more that evening.

A Long Way to Cork

THEY were spelling in the shade of a bush fence, or pile of cut scrub, or something, and Pat O'Brien had a place that ought've bin covered by his pants, or a patch; and it was in the sun with Pat's outlying regions. And Dave Regan had a burning-glass. Whispered Dave to his mate lazily:

"I'll pop the glass onter Pat, Joe, an' when he jumps you jump too, an' yell 'Snake!' "

"Uh-um," murmured Joe, and he reached carelessly for a new axe-handle, which he fingered abstractedly.

Joe rolled over very lazily on to his elbow, and applied the glass like a magnifying glass to a common print.

In a little while Pat got up like a nervous horse that had thought it was miles away from man, and alone, till suddenly yelled at. And his language was bad about bulldog ants. But at the same time, almost, Joe jumped up, yelled "Snake!" and started to slash the bushes with the axe-handle.

"Beggod, boys," said Pat, "I'm bit!"

They were all up now.

"I'm bit, boys; an' where ye can't tie it!"

Joe and Dave took him, one on each side, and started to run him on the track to Government House; but they hadn't gone far when, at the hurried suggestion of one of the others and clamorous approval of the rest (there were four others), they threw Pat on his flat, and knelt and sat on him while Dave cut the place with his pocket-knife, and squeezed out as much blood as he could.

Then they ran him on again, only stopping once to take more of his blood, till they got to the huts.

The storekeeper was absent after his horse, so they walked Pat up and down while the super opened the store with the wood axe, and handed out two bottles of brandy.

They gave Pat a long pull, gave two fresh men a nip, who relieved the pacers, and walked Pat up and down with a spurt, while

the rest had a nip to brace their nerves.

"It's a long way to Cork, boys," said Pat. "It's a long way to Cork."

They gave him another pull, and walked him up and down.

"I can feel it goin' through me like fire, boys," he said. "I can feel it going through me like fire. Can't ye tie up me roomp somehow? Take a twist on a bit of fincin' wire or something."

One of them picked up a piece of fencing wire, but dropped it hopelessly.

They gave him another pull, and walked him up and down. And every time they walked him up and down the others had nips to keep up their spirits.

"I'm drowsin' down, boys," he said, wearily. "I'm drowsin' down. Ah! boys, it's a pity to lose such a man."

They roused him up, and walked him up and down before giving him another pull, but they had nips themselves to keep up to it.

"Ah, boys!" he said. "It's a long way to Cork."

"So it seems," said the super; but he got out a couple more bottles to be ready. He had some himself. They gave Pat another pull, and walked him up and down. The relief had pulls before they went in, and the relieved had pulls when they fell out.

And they walked him up and down.

They started one off on horseback to Stiffner's, on the main road, to see if there was a doctor or snakebite expert there, and to bring back more spirits, in case they ran short. The super gave him two quid, but he never came back.

And they walked Pat up and down and did exactly as before, till they couldn't wake him, nor the super—nor themselves till next day.

Pat woke first, and thought, and remembered; then he roused Dave, and, staggering, walked *him* up and down.

"Dave," he said (in conclusion). "Dave, me friend. Ye saved me life wid ye're pocket-knife, and soocked me blood. Here's a couple of quid for ye're sweetheart, me boy. An' there's wan of the same again whinever and any time ye ask for it."

"Don't mention, Pat," said Dave. "It was nothing. I'd do the same to yer any day."

"I know ye would, me boy," said Pat, and, the super being still unconscious, they lay down again, well within the home gums' shade, and slept like brothers.

At Dead Dingo

I T was blazing hot outside and smothering hot inside the weatherboard and iron shanty at Dead Dingo, a place on the "cleared road", where there was a pub and a police station, and which was sometimes called "Roasted" and other times "Potted" Dingo—nicknames suggested by the everlasting drought and the vicinity of the one-pub township of Tinned Dog.

From the front veranda the scene was straight cleared road, running right and left to outback, and to Bourke (and ankle-deep in the red sand dust for perhaps a hundred miles); the rest blue-grey bush, dust, and the heat-wave blazing across every object.

There were only four in the bar-room, though it was New Year's Day. There weren't many more in the county. The girl sat behind the bar—the coolest place in the shanty—reading "Deadwood Dick". On a worn and torn and battered horsehair sofa, which had seen cooler places and better days, lay an awful and healthy example, a bearded swagman, with his arms twisted over his head and his face to the wall, sleeping off the death of the dead drunk. Bill and Jim—shearer and rouseabout—sat at a table playing cards. It was about three o'clock in the afternoon, and they had been gambling since nine—and the greater part of the night before—so they were, probably, in a worse condition morally (and perhaps physically) than the drunken swagman on the sofa.

Close under the bar, in a dangerous place for his legs and tail, lay a sheepdog with a chain attached to his collar and wound round his neck.

Presently a thump on the table, and Bill, unlucky gambler, rose with an oath that would have been savage if it hadn't been drawled.

"Stumped?" inquired Jim.

"Not a blanky, lurid deener!" drawled Bill.

Jim drew his reluctant hands from the cards, his eyes went slowly and hopelessly round the room and out the door. There was something in the eyes of both, except when on the card-table, of the look of a man waking in a strange place.

"Got anything?" asked Jim, fingering the cards again.

Bill sucked in his cheeks, collected the saliva with difficulty, and spat out on to the veranda floor.

"That's all I got," he drawled. "It's gone now."

Jim leaned back in his chair, twisted, yawned, and caught sight of the dog.

"That there dog yours?" he asked, brightening.

They had evidently been strangers the day before, or as strange to each other as bushmen can be.

Bill scratched behind his ear, and blinked at the dog. The dog woke suddenly to a flea fact.

"Yes," drawled Bill, "he's mine."

"Well, I'm going outback, and I want a dog," said Jim, gathering the cards briskly. "Half a quid agin the dog?"

"Half a quid be ——!" drawled Bill. "Call it a quid?"

"Half a blanky quid!"

"A gory, lurid quid!" drawled Bill desperately, and he stooped over his swag.

But Jim's hands were itching in a ghastly way over the cards.

"All right. Call it a —— quid."

The drunkard on the sofa stirred, showed signs of waking, but died again. Remember this, it might come in useful.

Bill sat down to the table once more.

Jim rose first, winner of the dog. He stretched, yawned "Ah, well!" and shouted drinks. Then he shouldered his swag, stirred the dog up with his foot, unwound the chain, said "Ah, well—so-long!" and drifted out and along the road towards outback, the dog following with head and tail down.

Bill scored another drink on account of girl-pity for bad luck, shouldered his swag, said "So-long, Mary!" and drifted out and along the road towards Tinned Dog, on the Bourke side. A long, drowsy half-hour passed—the sort of half-hour that is as long as an hour in the places where days are as long as years, and years hold about as much as days do in other places.

The man on the sofa woke with a start, and looked scared and wild for a moment; then he brought his dusty broken boots to the floor, rested his elbows on his knees, took his unfortunate head between his hands, and came back to life gradually.

He lifted his head, looked at the girl across the top of the bar, and formed with his lips, rather than spoke, the words:

"Put up a drink?"

She shook her head tightly and went on reading.

He staggered up, and leaning on the bar, made desperate distress signals with hand, eyes, and mouth.

"No!" she snapped. "I means no when I says no! You've had too many last drinks already, and the boss says you ain't to have another. If you swear again, or bother me, I'll call him."

He hung sullenly on the counter for a while, then lurched to his swag, and shouldered it hopelessly and wearily. Then he blinked round, whistled, waited a moment, went on to the front veranda, peered round through the heat with bloodshot eyes and whistled again. He turned and started through to the back door.

"What the devil do you want now?" demanded the girl, interrupted in her reading for the third time by him. "Stampin' all over the house. You can't go through there! It's privit! I do wish to goodness you'd git!"

"Where the blazes is that there dog o' mine got to?" he muttered. "Did you see a dog?"

"No! What do I want with your dog?"

He whistled out in front again, and round each corner. Then he came back with a decided step and tone.

"Look here! that there dog was lyin' there agin the wall when I went to sleep. He wouldn't stir from me, or my swag, in a year, if he wasn't dragged. He's been blanky well touched, and I wouldn'ter lost him for a fiver. Are you sure you ain't seen a dog?" Then suddenly, as the thought struck him: "Where's them two chaps that was playin' cards when I wenter sleep?"

"Why!" exclaimed the girl, without thinking, "there was a dog, now I come to think of it, but I thought it belonged to one of them chaps. Anyway, they played for it, and the other chap won it and took it away."

He stared at her blankly, with thunder gathering in the blankness.

"What sort of a dog was it?"

Dog described; the chain round the neck settled it.

He scowled at her darkly.

"Now, look here," he said, "you've allowed gamblin' in this bar —your boss has. You've got no right to let spielers gamble away a man's dog. Is a customer to lose his dog every time he has a doze to suit your boss? I'll go straight across to the police camp and put you away, and I don't care if you lose your licence. I ain't goin' to lose my dog. I wouldn'ter taken a ten-pound note for that blanky dog! I——"

She was filling a pewter hastily.

"Here! for God's sake have a drink an' stop yer row."

He drank with satisfaction. Then he hung on the bar with one elbow and scowled out the door.

"Which blanky way did them chaps go?" he growled.

"The one that took the dog went towards Tinned Dog."

"And I'll haveter go all the blanky way back after him, and most likely lose me shed! Here!" jerking the empty pewter across the bar, "fill that up again; I'm narked properly, I am, and I'll take twenty-four blanky hours to cool down now. I wouldn'ter lost that dog for twenty quid."

He drank again with deeper satisfaction, then he shuffled out, muttering, swearing, and threatening louder every step, and took the track to Tinned Dog.

Now the man, girl, or woman, who told me this yarn has never quite settled it in his or her mind as to who really owned the dog. I leave it to you.

A Bush Publican's Lament

. . . For thirst is long and throats is short
Among the sons o' men.

M.J.C.

I WISH I was spifflicated before I ever seen a pub!

You see, it's this way. Suppose a cove comes along on a blazin' hot day in the drought—an' *you* ought to know how hell-hot it can be out here—an' he dumps his swag in the corner of the bar; an' he turns round an' he ses ter me, "Look here, boss, I ain't got a lonely steever on me, an' God knows when I'll git one. I've tramped ten miles this mornin', an' I'll have ter tramp another ten afore tonight. I'm expectin' ter git on shearin' with ol' Baldy Thompson at West-o'-Sunday nex' week. I got a thirst on me like a sun-struck bone, an', for God sake, put up a couple o' beers for me an' my mate, an' I'll fix it up with yer when I come back after shearin'."

An' what's a feller ter do? I bin there meself, an'—I put it to you! I've known what it is to have a thirst on me.

An' suppose a poor devil comes along in the jim-jams, with every inch on him jumpin' an' a look in his eyes like a man bein' murdered an' sent ter hell, an' a whine in his voice like a whipped cur, an' the snakes a-chasing of him; an' he hooks me with his finger ter the far end o' the bar—as if he was goin' ter tell me that the world has ended—an' he hangs over the bar an' chews me lug, an' tries to speak, an' breaks off inter a sort o' low shriek, like a terrified woman, an' he says, "For Mother o' Christ's sake, giv' me a drink!" An' what am I to do? I bin there meself. I knows what the horrors is. He mighter blued his cheque at the last shanty. But what am I ter do? I put it ter you. If I let him go he might hang hisself ter the nex' leanin' tree.

What's a drink? yer might arst—I don't mind a drink or two; but when it comes to half a dozen in a day it mounts up, I can tell yer. Drinks is sixpence here—I have to pay for it, an' pay carriage on it. It's all up ter me in the end. I used sometimes ter think it was

"Endurable in his Sphere"

Endurable in his Sphere

lucky I wasn't west o' the sixpenny-line, where I'd lose a shillin' on every drink I give away.

An' supposen a sundowner comes along smokin' tea-leaves, an' ses ter me, "Look here, boss! me an' my mate ain't had a smoke for three days!" What's a man ter do? I put it ter you! I'm a heavy smoker meself, an' I've known what it is to be without a smoke on the track. But nailrod is ninepence a stick out here, an' I have ter pay carriage. It all mounts up, I can tell yer.

An' supposen Ole King Billy an' his ole black gin comes round at holiday time and squats on the veranda, an' blarneys an' whee-dles and whines and argues like a hundred Jews an' old Irishwomen put tergether, an' accuses me o' takin' his blarsted country from him, an' makes me an' the missus laugh; an' we gives him a bottl'er rum an' a bag of grub ter get rid of him an' his rotten old scarecrow tribe—it all tells up. I was allers soft on the blacks, an', beside, a ole gin nursed me an' me mother when I was born, an' saved me blessed life—not that that mounts to much. But it all tells up, an' I got me licence ter pay. An' some bloody skunk goes an' informs on me for supplyin' the haboriginalls with intossicatin' liquor, an' I have ter pay a fine an' risk me licence. But what's a man ter do?

An' three or four herrin'-gutted jackeroos comes along about dinner-time, when the table's set and the cookin' smellin' from the kitchen, with their belts done up three holes, an' not the price of a feed on 'em. What's a man ter do? I've known what it is ter do a perish on the track meself. It's not the tucker I think on. I don't care a damn for that. When the shearers come everyone is free to go inter the kitchin an' forage for hisself when he feels hungry—so long as he pays for his drinks. But the jackeroos can't pay for drinks, an' I have ter pay carriage on the flour an' tea an' sugar an' groceries—an' it all tells up by the end o' the year.

An' a straight chap that knows me gets a job to take a flock o' sheep or a mob o' cattle ter the bloomin' Gulf, or South Australia, or somewheers—an' loses one of his horses goin' out ter take charge, an' borrers eight quid from me ter buy another. He'll turn up agen in a year or two an' most likely want ter make me take twenty quid for that eight—an' make everybody about the place blind drunk—but I've got ter wait, an' the wine an' spirit merchants an' the brewery won't. They know I can't do without liquor in the place.

An' lars' rains Jimmy Nowlett, the bullock-driver, gets bogged over his axle-trees back there on the Blacksoil Plains between two flooded billerbongs, an' prays till the country steams an' his soul's busted, an' his throat like a lime-kiln. He taps a keg o' rum or beer ter keep his throat in workin' order. I don't mind that at all, but him an' his mates git flood-bound for a week, an' broach more kegs, an' go on a howlin' spree in ther mud, an' spill mor'n they swipe, an' leave a tarpaulin off a load, an' the flour gets wet, an' the sugar runs out of the bags like syrup, an'—What's a feller ter do? Do yer expect me to set the law onter Jimmy? I've knowed him all my life, an' he knowed my father afore I was born. He's been on the roads this forty year, till he's as thin as a rat, and as poor as a myall black; an' he's got a family ter keep back there in Bourke. No, I have ter pay for it in the end, an' it all mounts up, I can tell yer.

An' suppose some poor devil of a newchum black sheep comes along, staggerin' from one side of the track to the other, and spoutin' poetry; dyin' o' heat or fever, or heartbreak an' home-sickness, or a life o' disserpation he'd led in England, an' without a sprat on him, an' no claim on the bush; an' I ketches him in me arms as he stumbles inter the bar, an' he wants me ter hold him up while he turns English inter Greek for me. An' I put him ter bed, an' he gits worse, an' I have ter send the buggy twenty mile for a doctor—an' pay him. An' the jackeroo gits worse, an' has ter be watched an' nursed an' held down sometimes; an' he raves about his home an' mother in England, an' the blasted University that he was eddicated at—an' a woman—an' somethin' that sounds like poetry in French; an' he upsets my missus a lot, an' makes her blubber. An' he dies, an' I have ter pay a man ter bury him (an' knock up a sort o' fence round the grave arterwards ter keep the stock out), an' send the buggy agen for a parson, an'—Well, what's a man ter do? I couldn't let him wander away an' die like a dog in the scrub, an' be shoved underground like a dog, too, if his body was ever found. The Government might pay ter bury him, but there ain't never been a pauper funeral from my house yet, an' there won't be one if I can help it—except it be meself.

An' then there's the bother goin' through his papers to try an' find out who he was an' where his friends is. An' I have ter get the missus to write a letter to his people, an' we have ter make up lies about how he died ter make it easier for 'em. An' goin' through his letters, the missus comes across a portrait an' a locket of hair, an' letters from his mother an' sisters an' girl; an' they upset her, an' she blubbers agin, an' gits sentimental—like she useter long ago when we was first married.

There was one bit of poetry—I forgit it now—that that there jackeroo kep' sayin' over an' over agen till it buzzed in me head; an', weeks after, I'd ketch the missus mutterin' it to herself in the kitchin till I thought she was goin' ratty.

An' we gets a letter from the jackeroo's friends that puts us to a lot more bother. I hate havin' anythin' to do with letters. An' some-one's sure to say he was lambed down an' cleaned out an' poisoned with bad bush liquor at my place. It's almost enough ter make a man wish there *was* a recordin' angel.

An' what's the end of it? I got the blazin' bailiff in the place now! I can't shot him out because he's a decent, hard-up, poor devil from Bourke, with consumption or somethin', an' he's been talkin' to the missus about his missus an' kids; an' I see no chance of gittin' rid of him, unless the shearers come along with their cheques from West-o'-Sunday nex' week and act straight by me. Like as not I'll have ter roll up me swag an' take the track meself in the end. They say publicans are damned, an' I think so, too; an' I wish I'd bin operated on before ever I seen a pub.

The Geological Spieler

THERE's nothing so interesting as Geology, even to common and ignorant people, especially when you have a bank or the side of a cutting, studded with fossil fish and things and oysters that were stale when Adam was fresh, to illustrate by.

(Remark made by Steelman, professional wanderer, to his pal and pupil, Smith.)

THE first man that Steelman and Smith came up to on the last embankment, where they struck the new railway-line, was a heavy, gloomy, labouring man with bowyangs on and straps round his wrists. Steelman bade him the time of day and had a few words with him over the weather. The man of mullock gave it as his opinion that the fine weather wouldn't last, and seemed to take a gloomy kind of pleasure in that reflection; he said there was more rain down yonder, pointing to the south-east, than the moon could swallow up—the moon was in its first quarter, during which time it is popularly believed in some parts of Maori-land that the south-easter is most likely to be out on the wallaby and the weather bad. Steelman regarded that quarter of the sky with an expression of gentle remonstrance mingled, as it were, with a sort of fatherly indulgence, agreed mildly with the labouring man, and seemed lost for a moment in a reverie from which he roused himself to inquire cautiously after the boss. There was no boss, it was a co-operative party. That chap standing over there by the dray in the end of the cutting was their spokesman—their representative: they called him boss, but that was only his nickname in camp. Steelman expressed his thanks and moved on towards the cutting, followed respectfully by Smith.

Steelman wore a snuff-coloured sac suit, a wide-awake hat, a pair of professional-looking spectacles, and a scientific expression; there was a clerical atmosphere about him, strengthened, however, by an air as of unconscious dignity and superiority, born of intellect and knowledge. He carried a black bag, which was an indispensable article in his profession in more senses than one. Smith was decently dressed in sober tweed and looked like a man of no account who was mechanically devoted to his employer's interests, pleasures, or whims.

The boss was a decent-looking young fellow, with a good face—rather solemn—and a quiet manner.

"Good day, sir," said Steelman.

"Good day, sir," said the boss.

"Nice weather this."

"Yes, it is, but I'm afraid it won't last."

"I am afraid it will not by the look of the sky down there," ventured Steelman.

"No, I go mostly by the look of our weather prophet," said the boss with a quiet smile, indicating the gloomy man.

"I suppose bad weather would put you back in your work?"

"Yes, it will; we didn't want any bad weather just now."

Steelman got the weather question satisfactorily settled; then he said:

"You seem to be getting on with the railway."

"Oh yes, we are about over the worst of it."

"The worst of it?" echoed Steelman, with mild surprise. "I should have thought you were just coming into it," and he pointed to the ridge ahead.

"Oh, our section doesn't go any further than that pole you see sticking up yonder. We had the worst of it back there across the swamps—working up to our waists in water most of the time, in mid-winter too—and at eighteen-pence a yard."

"That was bad."

"Yes, rather rough. Did you come from the terminus?"

"Yes, I sent my baggage on in the brake."

"Commercial traveller, I suppose?" asked the boss, glancing at Smith, who stood a little to the rear of Steelman, seeming interested in the work.

"Oh no," said Steelman, smiling—"I am—well—I'm a geologist; this is my man here," indicating Smith. "You may put down the bag, James, and have a smoke. . . . My name is Stoneleigh—you might have heard it."

The boss said, "Oh," and then presently he added "Indeed," in an undecided tone.

There was a pause—embarrassed on the part of the boss—he was silent not knowing what to say. Meanwhile Steelman studied his man and concluded that he would do.

"Having a look at the country, I suppose?" asked the boss presently.

"Yes," said Steelman; then after a moment's reflection: "I am travelling for my own amusement and improvement, and also in the interests of science, which amounts to the same thing. I am a member of the Royal Geological Society—vice-president in fact of a leading Australian branch;" and then, as if conscious that he had appeared guilty of egotism, he shifted the subject a bit. "Yes. Very interesting country this—very interesting indeed. I should like to make a stay here for a day or so. Your work opens right into my hands. I cannot remember seeing a geological formation which interested me so much. Look at the face of that cutting, for instance. Why! you can almost read the history of the geological world from yesterday—this morning as it were—beginning with the super-surface and going right down through the different layers and stratas —through the vanished ages—right down and back to the pre-historical—to the very primeval or fundamental geological formations!" And Steelman studied the face of the cutting as if he could read it like a book, with every layer or stratum a chapter, and every streak a note of explanation. The boss seemed to be getting interested, and Steelman gained confidence and proceeded to identify and classify the different "stratas and layers", and fix their ages, and describe the conditions and politics of a man in their different times, for the boss's benefit.

"Now," continued Steelman, turning slowly from the cutting, removing his glasses, and letting his thoughtful eyes wander casually over the general scenery—"now the first impression that this country would leave on an ordinary intelligent mind—though maybe unconsciously, would be as of a new country—new in a geological sense; with patches of an older geological and vegetable formation cropping out here and there; as for instance that clump of dead trees on that clear alluvial slope there, that outcrop of limestone, or that timber yonder," and he indicated a dead forest which seemed alive and green because of the parasites. "But the country is old— old; perhaps the oldest geological formation in the world is to be seen here, the oldest vegetable formation in Australasia. I am not using the words old and new in an ordinary sense, you understand. but in a geological sense."

The boss said, "I understand," and that geology must be a very interesting study.

Steelman ran his eye meditatively over the cutting again, and turning to Smith said:

"Go up there, James, and fetch me a specimen of that slaty outcrop you see there—just above the coeval strata."

It was a stiff climb and slippery, but Smith had to do it, and he did it.

"This," said Steelman, breaking the rotten piece between his fingers, "belongs probably to an older geological period than its position would indicate—a primitive sandstone level perhaps. Its position on that layer is no doubt due to volcanic upheavals—such disturbances, or rather the results of such disturbances, have been and are the cause of the greatest trouble to geologists—endless errors and controversy. You see, we must study the country, not as it appears now, but as it would appear had the natural geological growth been left to mature undisturbed; we must restore and reconstruct such disorganized portions of the mineral kingdom, if you understand me."

The boss said he understood.

Steelman found an opportunity to wink sharply and severely at Smith, who had been careless enough to allow his features to relapse into a vacant grin.

"It is generally known even amongst the ignorant that rock grows—grows from the outside—but the rock here, a specimen of which I hold in my hand, is now in the process of decomposition; to be plain, it is rotting—in an advanced stage of decomposition—so much so that you are not able to identify it with any geological period or formation, even as you may not be able to identify any other extremely decomposed body."

The boss blinked and knitted his brow, but has the presence of mind to say: "Just so."

"Had the rock on that cutting been healthy—been alive, as it were—you would have had your work cut out; but it is dead and has been dead for ages perhaps. You find less trouble in working it than you would ordinary clay or sand, or even gravel, which formations together are really rock in embryo—before birth as it were."

The boss's brow cleared.

"The country round here is simply rotting down—simply rotting down."

He removed his spectacles, wiped them, and wiped his face; then his attention seemed to be attracted by some stones at his feet. He picked one up and examined it.

"I shouldn't wonder," he mused, absently, "I shouldn't wonder if there is alluvial gold in some of these creeks and gullies, perhaps tin or even silver, quite probably antimony."

The boss seemed interested.

"Can you tell me if there is any place in this neighbourhood where I could get accommodation for myself and my servant for a day or two?" asked Steelman presently. "I should very much like to break my journey here."

"Well, no," said the boss. "I can't say I do—I don't know of any place nearer than Pahiatua, and that's seven miles from here."

"I know that," said Steelman reflectively, "but I fully expected to have found a house or accommodation of some sort on the way, else I would have gone on in the van."

"Well," said the boss, "if you like to camp with us for tonight, at least, and don't mind roughing it, you'll be welcome, I'm sure."

"If I was sure that I would not be putting you to any trouble, or interfering in any way with your domestic economy——"

"No trouble at all," interrupted the boss. "The boys will be only too glad, and there's an empty whare where you can sleep. Better stay. It's going to be a rough night."

After tea Steelman entertained the boss and a few of the more thoughtful members of the party with short chatty lectures on geology and other subjects.

In the meantime Smith, in another part of the camp, gave selections on a tin whistle, sang a song or two, contributed, in his turn, to the sailor yarns, and ensured his popularity for several nights at least. After several draughts of something that was poured out of a demijohn into a pint-pot, his tongue became loosened, and he expressed an opinion that geology was all bosh, and said if he had half his employer's money he'd be dashed if he would go rooting round in the mud like a blessed old ant-eater; he also irreverently referred to his learned boss as "Old Rocks over there". He had a pretty easy billet of it though, he said, taking it all round, when the weather was fine; he got a couple of notes a week and all expenses paid, and the money was sure; he was only required to look after the luggage and arrange for accommodation, grub out a chunk of rock now and then, and (what perhaps was the most irksome of his duties) he had to appear interested in old rocks and clay.

Towards midnight Steelman and Smith retired to the unoccupied whare which had been shown them, Smith carrying a bundle of bags, blankets, and rugs, which had been placed at their disposal by their good-natured hosts. Smith lit a candle and proceeded to make the beds. Steelman sat down, removed his specs and scientific expression, placed the glasses carefully on a ledge close at hand, took a book from his bag, and commenced to read. The volume was a cheap copy of Jules Verne's *Journey to the Centre of the Earth*. A little later there was a knock at the door. Steelman hastily resumed the spectacles, together with the scientific expression, took a notebook from his pocket, opened it on the table, and said, "Come in." One of the chaps appeared with a billy of hot coffee, two pint-pots, and some cake. He said he thought you chaps might like a drop of coffee before you turned in, and the boys forgot to ask you to wait for it down in the camp. He also wanted to know whether Mr Stoneleigh and his man would be all right and quite comfortable for the night, and whether they had blankets enough. There was some wood at the back of the whare and they could light a fire if they liked.

Mr Stoneleigh expressed his thanks and his appreciation of the kindness shown him and his servant. He was extremely sorry to give them any trouble.

The navvy, a serious man, who respected genius or intellect in any shape or form, said that it was no trouble at all, the camp was very dull and the boys were always glad to have someone come round. Then, after a brief comparison of opinions concerning the probable duration of the weather which had arrived, they bade each other good night, and the darkness swallowed the serious man.

Steelman turned into the top bunk on one side and Smith took the lower on the other. Steelman had the candle by his bunk, as usual; he lit his pipe for a final puff before going to sleep, and held the light up for a moment so as to give Smith the full benefit of a solemn, uncompromising wink. The wink was silently applauded and dutifully returned by Smith. Then Steelman blew out the light, lay back, and puffed at his pipe for a while. Presently he chuckled, and the chuckle was echoed by Smith; by and by Steelman chuckled once more, and then Smith chuckled again. There was silence in the darkness, and after a bit Smith chuckled twice. Then Steelman said:

"For God's sake give her a rest, Smith, and give a man a show to get some sleep."

Then the silence in the darkness remained unbroken.

The invitation was extended next day, and Steelman sent Smith on to see that his baggage was safe. Smith stayed out of sight for two or three hours, and then returned and reported all well.

They stayed on for several days. After breakfast and when the men were going to work Steelman and Smith would go out along the line with the black bag and poke round amongst the "layers and stratas" in sight of the works for a while, as an evidence of good faith; then they'd drift off casually into the bush, camp in a retired and sheltered spot, and light a fire when the weather was cold, and Steelman would lie on the grass and read and smoke and lay plans for the future and improve Smith's mind until they reckoned it was about dinner-time. And in the evening they would come home with the black bag full of stones and bits of rock, and Steelman would lecture on those minerals after tea.

On about the fourth morning Steelman had a yarn with one of the men going to work. He was a lanky young fellow with a sandy complexion, and seemingly harmless grin. In Australia he might have been regarded as a "cove" rather than a "chap", but there was nothing of the "bloke" about him. Presently the cove said:

"What do you think of the boss, Mr Stoneleigh? He seems to have taken a great fancy for you, and he's fair gone on geology."

"I think he is a very decent fellow indeed, a very intelligent young man. He seems very well read and well informed."

"You wouldn't think he was a University man," said the cove.

"No, indeed! Is he?"

"Yes. I thought you knew!"

Steelman knitted his brows. He seemed slightly disturbed for the moment. He walked on a few paces in silence and thought hard.

"What might have been his special line?" he asked the cove.

"Why, something the same as yours. I thought you knew. He was reckoned the best—what do you call it?—the best minrologist in the country. He had a first-class billet in the Mines Department, but he lost it—you know—the booze."

"I think we will be making a move, Smith," said Steelman, later on, when they were private. "There's a little too much intellect in this camp to suit me. But we haven't done so bad, anyway. We've had three days' good board and lodging with entertainments and refreshments thrown in." Then he said to himself: "We'll stay for another day anyway. If those beggars are having a lark with us, we're getting the worth of it anyway, and I'm not thin-skinned. They're the mugs and not us, anyhow it goes, and I can take them down before I leave."

But on the way home he had a talk with another man whom we might set down as a "chap".

"I would have thought the boss was a college man," said Steelman to the chap.

"A what?"

"A University man—University education."

"Why! Who's been telling you that?"

"One of your mates."

"Oh, he's been getting at you. Why, it's all the boss can do to write his own name. Now that lanky sandy cove with the birthmark grin—it's him that's had the college education."

"I think we'll make a start tomorrow," said Steelman to Smith in the privacy of their whare. "There's too much humour and levity in this camp to suit a serious scientific gentleman like myself."

Poisonous Jimmy Gets Left

"WHEN we got tired of digging about Mudgee-Budgee, and getting no gold," said Dave Regan, bushman, "me and my mate, Jim Bently, decided to take a turn at droving; so we went with Bob Baker, the drover, overland with a big mob of cattle, way up into northern Queensland.

"We couldn't get a job on the home track, and we spent most of our money, like a pair of fools, at a pub at a town way up over the border, where they had a flash barmaid from Brisbane. We sold our packhorses and pack-saddles, and rode out of that town with our swags on our riding-horses in front of us. We had another spree at another place, and by the time we got near New South Wales we were pretty well stumped.

"Just the other side of Mulgatown, near the border, we came on a big mob of cattle in a paddock, and a party of drovers camped on the creek. They had brought the cattle down from the north and were going no farther with them; their boss had ridden on into Mulgatown to get the cheques to pay them off, and they were waiting for him.

"'And Poisonous Jimmy is waiting for us,' said one of them.

"Poisonous Jimmy kept a shanty a piece along the road from their camp towards Mulgatown. He was called Poisonous Jimmy perhaps on account of his liquor, or perhaps because he had a job of poisoning dingoes on a station in the Bogan scrubs at one time. He was a sharp publican. He had a girl, and they said that whenever a shearing-shed cut out on his side and he saw the shearers coming along the road, he'd say to the girl, 'Run and get your best frock on, Mary! Here's the shearers comin'.' And if a cheque-man wouldn't drink he'd try to get him into his bar and shout for him till he was too drunk to keep his hands out of his pockets.

"'But he won't get us,' said another of the drovers. 'I'm going to ride straight into Mulgatown and send my money home by the post as soon as I get it.'

" 'You've always said that, Jack,' said the first drover.

"We yarned a while, and had some tea, and then me and Jim got on our horses and rode on. We were burned to bricks and ragged and dusty and parched up enough, and so were our horses. We only had a few shillings to carry us four or five hundred miles home, but it was mighty hot and dusty, and we felt that we must have a drink at the shanty. This was west of the sixpenny-line at that time—all drinks were a shilling along here.

"Just before we reached the shanty I got an idea.

" 'We'll plant our swags in the scrub,' I said to Jim.

" 'What for?' said Jim.

" 'Never mind—you'll see,' I said.

"So we unstrapped our swags and hid them in the mulga scrub by the side of the road; then we rode on to the shanty, got down, and hung our horses to the veranda-posts.

"Poisonous came out at once, with a smile on him that would have made anybody homesick.

"He was a short nuggety man, and could use his hands, they said; he looked as if he'd be a nasty, vicious, cool customer in a fight— he wasn't the sort of man you'd care to try and swindle a second time. He had a monkey shave when he shaved, but now it was all frill and stubble—like a bush fence round a stubble-field. He had a broken nose, and a cunning, sharp, suspicious eye that squinted, and a cold stoney eye that seemed fixed. If you didn't know him well you might talk to him for five minutes, looking at him in the cold stoney eye, and then discover that it was the sharp cunning little eye that was watching you all the time. It was awful embarrassing. It must have made him awkward to deal with in a fight.

" 'Good day, mates,' he said.

" 'Good day,' we said.

" 'It's hot.'

" 'It's hot.'

"We went into the bar, and Poisonous got behind the counter.

" 'What are you going to have?' he asked, rubbing up his glasses with a rag.

"We had two long beers.

" 'Never mind that,' said Poisonous, seeing me put my hand in my pocket; 'it's my shout. I don't suppose your boss is back yet? I saw him go into Mulgatown this morning.'

"'No, he ain't back,' I said: 'I wish he was. We're getting tired of waiting for him. We'll give him another hour, and then some of us will have to ride in to see whether he's got on the booze, and get hold of him if he has.'

"'I suppose you're waiting for your cheques?' he said, turning to fix some bottles on the shelf.

"'Yes,' I said, 'we are', and I winked at Jim, and Jim winked back as solemn as an owl.

"Poisonous asked us all about the trip, and how long we'd been on the track, and what sort of a boss we had, dropping the questions offhand now an' then, as for the sake of conversation. We could see that he was trying to get at the size of our supposed cheques, so we answered accordingly.

"'Have another drink,' he said, and he filled the pewters up again. 'It's up to me,' and he set to work boring out the glasses with his rag, as if he was short-handed and the bar was crowded with customers, and screwing up his face into what I suppose he considered an innocent or unconscious expression. The girl began to sidle in and out with a smart frock and a see-you-after-dark smirk on.

"'Have you had dinner?' she asked. We could have done with a good meal, but it was too risky—the drovers' boss might come along while we were at dinner and get into conversation with Poisonous. So we said we'd had dinner.

"Poisonous filled our pewters again in an offhand way.

"'I wish the boss would come,' said Jim with a yawn. 'I want to get into Mulgatown tonight, and I want to get some shirts and things before I go in. I ain't got a decent rag to me back. I don't suppose there's ten bob amongst the lot of us.'

"There was a general store back on the creek, near the drovers' camp.

"'Oh, go to the store and get what you want,' said Poisonous, taking a sovereign from the till and tossing it on to the counter. 'You can fix it up with me when your boss comes. Bring your mates along.'

"'Thank you,' said Jim, taking up the sovereign carelessly and dropping it into his pocket.

"'Well, Jim,' I said, 'suppose we get back to camp and see how the chaps are getting on?'

"'All right,' said Jim.

"'Tell them to come down and get a drink,' said Poisonous; 'or, wait, you can take some beer along to them if you like,' and he gave us half a gallon of beer in a billy-can. He knew what the first drink meant with bushmen back from a long dry trip.

"We got on our horses, I holding the billy very carefully, and rode back to where our swags were.

"'I say,' said Jim, when we'd strapped the swags to the saddles, 'suppose we take the beer back to those chaps: it's meant for them, and it's only a fair thing, anyway—we've got as much as we can hold till we get into Mulgatown.'

"'It might get them into a row,' I said, 'and they seem decent chaps. Let's hang the billy on a twig, and that old swagman that's coming along will think there's angels in the bush.'

"'Oh, what's a row?' said Jim. 'They can take care of themselves; they'll have the beer anyway and a lark with Poisonous when they take the can back and it comes to explanations. I'll ride back to them.'

"So Jim rode back to the drovers' camp with the beer, and when he came back to me he said that the drovers seemed surprised, but they drank good luck to him.

"We rode round through the mulga behind the shanty and came out on the road again on the Mulgatown side: we only stayed at Mulgatown to buy some tucker and tobacco, then we pushed on and camped for the night about seven miles on the safe side of the town."

An Oversight of Steelman's

STEELMAN and Smith—professional wanderers—were making back for Wellington, down through the wide and rather dreary-looking Hutt Valley. They were broke. They carried their few remaining belongings in two skimpy, amateurish-looking swags. Steelman had fourpence left. They were very tired and very thirsty—at least Steelman was, and he answered for both. It was Smith's policy to feel and think just exactly as Steelman did. Said Steelman:

"The landlord of the next pub is not a bad sort. I won't go in—he might remember me. You'd best go in. You've been tramping round in the Wairarapa district for the last six months, looking for work. You're going back to Wellington now, to try and get on the new corporation works just being started there—the sewage works. You think you've got a show. You've got some mates in Wellington, and they're looking out for a chance for you. You did get a job last week on a sawmill at Silverstream, and the boss sacked you after three days and wouldn't pay you a penny. That's just his way. I know him—at least a mate of mine does. I've heard of him often enough. His name's Cowman. Don't forget the name, whatever you do. The landlord here hates him like poison; he'll sympathize with you. Tell him you've got a mate with you; he's gone ahead—took a short cut across the paddocks. Tell him you've got only fourpence left, and see if he'll give you a drop in a bottle. Says you: 'Well, boss, the fact is we've only got fourpence, but you might let us have a drop in a bottle;' and very likely he'll stand you a couple of pints in a gin-bottle. You can fling the coppers on the counter, but the chances are he won't take them. He's not a bad sort. Beer's fourpence a pint out here, same's in Wellington. See that gin-bottle lying there by the stump; get it and we'll take it down to the river with us and rinse it out."

They reached the river-bank.

"You'd better take my swag—it looks more decent," said Steelman. "No, I'll tell you what we'll do: we'll undo both swags and make them into one—one decent swag, and I'll cut round through

Wayfaring Diggers
La Trobe Library, State Library of Victoria

the lanes and wait for you on the road ahead of the pub."

He rolled up the swag with much care and deliberation and considerable judgment. He fastened Smith's belt round one end of it, and the handkerchiefs round the other, and made a towel serve as a shoulder-strap.

"I wish we had a canvas bag to put it in," he said, "or a cover of some sort. But never mind. The landlord's an old Australian bushman, now I come to think of it; the swag looks Australian enough, and it might appeal to his feelings, you know—bring up old recollections. But you'd best not say you come from Australia, because he's been there, and he'd soon trip you up. He might have been where you've been, you know, so don't try to do too much. You always do mug-up the business when you try to do more than I tell you. You might tell him your mate came from Australia—but no, he might want you to bring me in. Better stick to Maoriland. I don't believe in too much ornamentation. Plain lies are the best."

"What's the landlord's name?" asked Smith.

"Never mind that. You don't want to know that. You are not supposed to know him at all. It might look suspicious if you called him by his name, and lead to awkward questions; then you'd be sure to put your foot into it."

"I could say I read it over the door."

"Bosh. Travellers don't read the names over the doors, when they go into pubs. You're an entire stranger to him, call him 'boss'. Say 'Good day, boss,' when you go in, and swing down your swag as if you're used to it. Ease it down like this. Then straighten yourself up, stick your hat back, and wipe your forehead, and try to look as hearty and independent and cheerful as you possibly can. Curse the Government, and say the country's done. It don't matter what Government it is, for he's always against it. I never knew a real Australian that wasn't. Say that you're thinking about trying to get over to Australia, and then listen to him talking about it—and try to look interested, too! Get that damned stone-deaf expression off your face! . . . He'll run Australia down most likely—I never knew an Othersider that had settled down over here who didn't. But don't you make any mistake and agree with him, because, although successful Australians over here like to run their own country down, there's very few of them that care to hear anybody else do it. . . . Don't come away as soon as you get your beer. Stay and listen to him for a while, as if you're interested in his yarning, and give him time to put you on to a job, or offer you one. Give him a chance to ask how you and your mate are off for tobacco or tucker. Like as not he'll sling you half a crown when you come away—that is, if you work it all right. Now try to think of something to say to him, and make yourself a bit interesting—if you possibly can. Tell him about the fight we saw back at the pub the other day. He might know some of the chaps. This is a sleepy hole, and there ain't much news knocking round. . . . I wish I could go in myself, but he's sure to remember me. I'm afraid he got left the last time I stayed there (so did one or two others); and, besides, I came away without saying good-bye to him, and he might feel a bit sore about it. That's the worst of travelling on the old road. Come on now, wake up!"

"Bet I'll get a quart," said Smith, brightening up, "and some tucker for it to wash down."

"If you don't," said Steelman, "I'll stoush you. Never mind the bottle; fling it away. It doesn't look well for a traveller to go into a pub with an empty bottle in his hand. A real swagman never does. It looks much better to come out with a couple of full ones. That's what you've got to do. Now, come along."

Steelman turned off into a lane, cut across the paddocks to the road again, and waited for Smith. He hadn't long to wait.

Smith went on towards the public-house, rehearsing his part as he walked—repeating his "lines" to himself, so as to be sure of remembering all that Steelman had told him to say to the landlord, and adding, with what he considered appropriate gestures, some fancy touches of his own, which he determined to throw in in spite of Steelman's advice and warning. "I'll tell him (this)—I'll tell him (that). Well, look here, boss, I'll say you're pretty right and I quite agree with you as far as that's concerned, but," etc. And so, murmuring and mumbling to himself, Smith reached the hotel. The day was late, and the bar was small, and low, and dark. Smith walked in with all the assurance he could muster, eased down his swag in a corner in what he no doubt considered the true professional style, and, swinging round to the bar, said in a loud voice which he intended to be cheerful, independent, and hearty:

"Good day, boss!"

But it wasn't a "boss". It was about the hardest-faced old woman that Smith had ever seen. The pub had changed hands.

"I—I beg your pardon, missus," stammered poor Smith.

It was a knock-down blow for Smith. He couldn't come to in

time. He and Steelman had had a landlord in their minds all the time, and laid their plans accordingly; the possibility of having a she—and one like this—to deal with never entered into their calculations. Smith had no time to reorganize, even if he had had the brains to do so without the assistance of his mate's knowledge of human nature.

"I—I beg your pardon, missus," he stammered.

Painful pause. She sized him up.

"Well, what do you want?"

"Well, missus—I—the fact is—will you give me a bottle of beer for fourpence?"

"Wha—what?"

"I mean——the fact is, we've only got fourpence left, and—I've got a mate outside, and you might let us have a quart or so, in a bottle, for that. I mean—anyway, you might let us have a pint. I'm very sorry to bother you, missus."

But she couldn't do it. No. Certainly not. Decidedly not! All her drinks were sixpence. She had her licence to pay, and the rent, and a family to keep. It wouldn't pay out there—it wasn't worth her while. It wouldn't pay the cost of carting the liquor out, etc.

"Well, missus," poor Smith blurted out at last, in sheer desperation, "give me what you can in a bottle for this. I've—I've got a mate outside." And he put the four coppers on the bar.

"Have you got a bottle?"

"No—but——"

"If I give you one, will you bring it back? You can't expect me to give you a bottle as well as a drink."

"Yes, mum; I'll bring it back directly."

She reached out a bottle from under the bar, and very deliberately measured out a little over a pint and poured it into the bottle, which she handed to Smith without a cork.

Smith went his way without rejoicing. It struck him forcibly that he should have saved the money until they reached Petone, or the city, where Steelman would be sure to get a decent drink. But how was he to know? He had chanced it, and lost; Steelman might have done the same. What troubled Smith most was the thought of what Steelman would say; he already heard him, in imagination, saying: "You're a mug, Smith—Smith, you *are* a mug."

But Steelman didn't say much. He was prepared for the worst by seeing Smith come along so soon. He listened to his story with an

air of gentle sadness, even as a stern father might listen to the volun-
tary confession of a wayward child; then he held the bottle up to
the fading light of departing day, looked through it (the bottle),
and said:

"Well—it ain't worth while dividing it."

Smith's heart shot right down through a hole in the sole of his
left boot into the hard road.

"Here, Smith," said Steelman, handing him the bottle, "drink
it, old man; you want it. It wasn't altogether your fault; it was an
oversight of mine. I didn't bargain for a woman of that kind, and,
of course, *you* couldn't be expected to think of it. Drink it! Drink
it down, Smith. I'll manage to work the oracle before this night is
out."

Smith was forced to believe his ears, and, recovering from his
surprise, drank.

"I promised to take back the bottle," he said, with the ghost of
a smile.

Steelman took the bottle by the neck and broke it on the fence.

"Come on, Smith; I'll carry the swag for a while."

And they tramped on in the gathering starlight.

The Darling River

THE Darling—which is either a muddy gutter or a second Mississippi—is about six times as long as the distance, in a straight line, from its head to its mouth. The state of the river is vaguely but generally understood to depend on some distant and foreign phenomena to which bushmen refer in an offhand tone of voice as "the Queenslan' rains", which seem to be held responsible, in a general way, for most of the outback trouble.

It takes less than a year to go up-stream by boat to Walgett or Bourke in a dry season; but after the first three months the passengers generally go ashore and walk. They get sick of being stuck in the same sort of place, in the same old way; they grow weary of seeing the same old whaler drop his swag on the bank opposite whenever the boat ties up for wood; they get tired of lending him tobacco, and listening to his ideas, which are limited in number and narrow in conception.

It shortens the journey to get out and walk; but then you will have to wait so long for your luggage—unless you hump it with you.

We heard of a man who determined to stick to a Darling boat and travel the whole length of the river. He was a newspaper man. He started on his voyage of discovery one Easter in flood-time, and a month later the captain got bushed between the Darling and South Australian border. The waters went away before he could find the river again, and left his boat in a scrub. They had a cargo of rations, and the crew stuck to the craft while the tucker lasted; when it gave out they rolled up their swags and went to look for a station, but didn't find one. The captain would study his watch and the sun, rig up dials and make out courses, and follow them without success. They ran short of water, and didn't smell any for weeks; they suffered terrible privations, and lost three of their number, *not* including the newspaper liar. There were even dark hints of considering the drawing of lots in connection with something too terrible to mention. They crossed a thirty-mile plain at last, and sighted a black gin. She led them to a boundary-rider's

95

hut, where they were taken in and provided with rations and rum.

Later on a syndicate was formed to explore the country and re-cover the boat; but they found her thirty miles from the river and about eighteen from the nearest waterhole deep enough to float her, so they left her there. She's there still, or else the man that told us about it is the greatest liar outback.

Imagine the hull of a North Shore ferry-boat, blunted a little at the ends and cut off about a foot below the water-line, and parallel to it, then you will have something shaped somewhat like the hull of a Darling mud-rooter. But the river boat is much stronger. The boat we were on was built and repaired above deck after the different ideas of many bush carpenters, of whom the last seemed by his work to have regarded the original plan with a contempt only equalled by his disgust at the work of the last carpenter but one. The wheel was boxed in, mostly with round sapling-sticks fastened to the frame with bunches of nails and spikes of all shapes and sizes, most of them bent. The general result was decidedly pictur-esque in its irregularity, but dangerous to the mental welfare of any passenger who was foolish enough to try to comprehend the design; for it seemed as though every carpenter had taken the opportunity to work in a little abstract idea of his own.

The way they dock a Darling River boat is beautiful for its sim-plicity. They choose a place where there are two stout trees about the boat's length apart, and standing on a line parallel to the river. They fix pulley-blocks to the trees, lay sliding planks down into the water, fasten a rope to one end of the steamer, and take the other end through the block attached to the tree and thence back aboard a second steamer; then they carry a rope similarly from the other end through the block on the second tree, and aboard a third boat. At a given signal one boat leaves for Wentworth, and the other starts for the Queensland border. The consequence is that craft number one climbs the bank amid the cheers of the local loafers, who congregate and watch the proceedings with great interest and approval. The crew pitch tents, and set to work on the hull, which looks like a big, rough shallow box.

We once travelled on the Darling for a hundred miles or so on a boat called the *Mud Turtle*—at least, that's what *we* called her. She might reasonably have haunted the Mississippi fifty years ago. She didn't seem particular where she went, or whether she started again or stopped for good after getting stuck. Her machinery sounded like a chapter of accidents and was always out of order, but she got along all the same, provided the steersman kept her off the bank.

Her skipper was a young man, who looked more like a drover than a sailor, and the crew bore a greater resemblance to the unemployed than to any other body we know of, except that they looked a little more independent. They seemed clannish, too, with an unemployed or free-labour sort of isolation. We have an idea that they regarded our personal appearance with contempt.

Above Louth we picked up a whaler, who came aboard for the sake of society and tobacco. Not that he hoped to shorten his journey. He had no destination. He told us many reckless and unprincipled lies, and gave us a few ornamental facts. One of them took our fancy, and impressed us—with its beautiful simplicity, I suppose. He said: "Some miles above where the Darlin' and the Warrygo runs inter each other there's a billygong runnin' right across between the two rivers and makin' a sort of tryhangular hyland; 'n' I can tel'yer a funny thing about it." Here he paused to light his pipe. "Now," he continued impressively, jerking the match overboard, "when the Darlin's up, and the Warrygo's low, the billygong runs from the Darlin' into the *Warrygo*; and, when the Warrygo's up 'n' the Darlin's down, the waters runs *from* the Warrygo 'n' inter the Darlin'."

What could be more simple?

The steamer was engaged to go up a billabong for a load of shearers from a shed which was cutting out; and first it was necessary to tie up in the river and discharge the greater portion of the cargo in order that the boat might safely negotiate the shallow waters. A local fisherman, who volunteered to act as pilot, was taken aboard, and after he was outside about a pint of whisky he seemed to have the greatest confidence in his ability to take us to hell, or anywhere else—at least, he said so. A man was sent ashore with blankets and tucker, to mind the wool, and we crossed the river, butted into the anabranch, and started outback. Only the Lord and the pilot know how we got there. We travelled over the bush, through its branches sometimes, and sometimes through grass and mud, and every now and then we struck something that felt and sounded like a collision. The boat slid down one hill, and "fetched"

97

a stump at the bottom with a force that made every mother's son bite his tongue or break a tooth.

The shearers came aboard next morning, with their swags and two cartloads of boiled mutton, bread, brownie, and tea and sugar. They numbered about fifty, including the rouseabouts. This load of sin sank the steamer deeper into the mud; but the passengers crowded over to port, by request of the captain, and the crew poked the bank away with long poles. When we began to move the shearers gave a howl like the yell of a legion of lost souls escaping from down below. They gave three cheers for the rouseabouts' cook, who stayed behind; then they cursed the station with a mighty curse. They cleared a space on deck, had a jig, and afterwards a fight between the shearer's cook and his assistant. They gave a mighty bush whoop for the Darling when the boat swung into that grand old gutter, and in the evening they had a general all-round time. We got back, and the crew had to reload the wool without assistance, for it bore the accursed brand of a freedom-of-contract shed.

We slept, or tried to sleep, that night on the ridge of two woolbales laid with the narrow sides up, having first been obliged to get ashore and fight six rounds with a shearer for the privilege of roosting there. The live cinders from the firebox went up the chimney all night, and fell in showers on deck. Every now and again a spark would burn through the Wagga rug of a sleeping shearer, and he'd wake suddenly and get up and curse. It was no use shifting round, for the wind was all ways, and the boat steered north, south, east, and west to humour the river. Occasionally a low branch would root three or four passengers off their wool-bales, and they'd get up and curse in chorus. The boat started two snags; and towards daylight struck a stump. The accent was on the stump. A wool-bale went overboard, and took a swag and a dog with it; then the owner of the swag and dog and the crew of the boat had a swearing match between them. The swagman won.

About daylight we stretched our cramped limbs, extricated one leg from between the wool-bales, and found that the steamer was just crayfishing away from a mud island, where she had tied up for more wool. Some of the chaps had been ashore and boiled four or five buckets of tea and coffee. Shortly after the boat had settled down to work again an incident came along. A rouseabout rose late, and, while the others were at breakfast, got an idea into his head that a good "sloosh" would freshen him up; so he mooched round until he found a big wooden bucket with a rope to it. He carried the bucket aft of the wheel. The boat was butting up-stream for all she was worth, and the stream was running the other way, of course, and about a hundred times as fast as a train. The jack-eroo gave the line a turn round his wrist; before anyone could see him in time to suppress him, he lifted the bucket, swung it to and fro, and dropped it cleverly into the water.

This delayed us for nearly an hour. A couple of men jumped into the rowboat immediately and cast her adrift. They picked up the jackeroo about a mile down the river, clinging to a snag, and when we hauled him aboard he looked like something the cat had dragged in, only bigger. We revived him with rum and got him on his feet; and then, when the captain and crew had done cursing him, he rubbed his head, went forward, and had a look at the paddle; then he rubbed his head again, thought, and remarked to his mates:

"Wasn't it lucky I didn't dip that bucket *for'ard* the wheel?"

This remark struck us forcibly. We agreed that it was lucky—for him; but the captain remarked that it was damned unlucky for the world, which, he explained, was over-populated with fools already.

Getting on towards afternoon we found a barge loaded with wool and tied up to a tree in the wilderness. There was no sign of a man to be seen, nor any sign, except the barge, that a human being had ever been there. The captain took the craft in tow, towed it about ten miles up the stream, and left it in a less likely place than where it was before.

Floating bottles began to be more frequent, and we knew by that same token that we were nearing "Here's Luck!"—Bourke, we mean. And this reminds us.

When the Brewarrina people observe a more than ordinary num-ber of bottles floating down the river, they guess that Walgett is on the spree; when the Louth chaps see an unbroken procession of dead marines for three or four days they know that Bourke's drunk. The poor, God-abandoned whaler sits in his hungry camp at sunset and watches the empty symbols of hope go by, and feels more God-forgotten than ever—and thirstier, if possible—and gets a great, wide, thirsty, quaking, empty longing to be up where those bottles come from. If the townspeople knew how much misery they caused by their thoughtlessness they would drown their dead marines, or bury them, but on no account allow them to go drifting down the river, and stirring up hells in the bosoms of less fortunate fellow-creatures.

There came a man from Adelaide to Bourke, once, and he collected all the empty bottles in town, stacked them by the river, and waited for a boat. What he wanted them for the legend sayeth not, but the people reckoned he had a private still, or something of that sort, somewhere down the river, and were satisfied. What he came from Adelaide for, or whether he really did come from there, we do not know. All the Darling bunyips are supposed to come from Adelaide. Anyway, the man collected all the empty bottles he could lay his hands on, and piled them on the bank, where they made a good show. He waited for a boat to take his cargo, and, while waiting, he got drunk. That excited no comment. He stayed drunk for three weeks, but the townspeople saw nothing unusual in that. In order to become an object of interest in their eyes, and in that line, he would have had to stay drunk for a year and fight three times a day—oftener, if possible—and lie in the road in the broiling heat between whiles, and be walked on by camels and Afghans and free-labourers, and be locked up every time he got sober enough to smash a policeman, and try to hang himself naked, and be finally squashed by a loaded wool-team.

But while he drank, the Darling rose, for reasons best known to itself, and floated those bottles off. They strung out and started for the Antarctic Ocean, with a big old wicker-worked demijohn in the lead.

For the first week the down-river men took no notice; but after the bottles had been drifting past with scarcely a break for a fortnight or so, they began to get interested. Several whalers watched the procession until they got the jim-jams by force of imagination, and when their bodies began to float down with the bottles, the down-river people got anxious.

At last the mayor of Wilcannia wired Bourke to know whether Dibbs or Parkes was dead, or democracy triumphant, or if not, wherefore the jubilation? Many telegrams of a like nature were received during that week, and the true explanation was sent in reply to each. But it wasn't believed, and to this day Bourke has the name of being the most drunken town on the river.

After dinner a humorous old hard case mysteriously took us aside and said he had a good yarn which we might be able to work up. We asked him how, but he winked a mighty cunning wink and said that he knew all about us. Then he asked us to listen. He said:

"There was an old feller down the Murrumbidgee named Kelly. He was a bit gone here. One day Kelly was out lookin' for some sheep, when he got lost. It was gettin' dark. Byemby there came an old crow in a tree overhead.

"'Kel-ley, you're lo-o-st! Kel-ley, you're lo-o-st!' sez the crow.

"'I know I am,' sez Kelly.

"'Fol-ler me, fol-ler me,' sez the crow.

"'Right y'are,' sez Kelly, with a jerk of his arm. 'Go ahead.'

"So the crow went on, and Kelly follered, an' byemby he found he was on the right track.

"Sometime after Kelly was washin' sheep (this was when we useter wash the sheep instead of the wool). Kelly was standin' on the platform with a crutch in his hand landin' the sheep, when there came a old crow in the tree overhead.

"'Kelly, I'm hun-gry! Kel-ley, I'm hun-ger-ry!' sez the crow.

"'All right,' sez Kelly; 'be up at the hut about dinner-time 'n' I'll sling you out something.'

"'Drown—a—sheep! Drown—a—sheep, Kel-ley,' sez the crow.

"'Blanked if I do,' sez Kelly. 'If I drown a sheep I'll have to pay for it, be-God!'

"'Then I won't find yer when yer lost agin,' sez the crow.

"'I'm damned if yer will,' says Kelly. 'I'll take blanky good care I won't get lost again, to be found by a gory ole crow.'"

There are a good many fishermen on the Darling. They camp along the banks in all sorts of tents, and move about in little box boats that will only float one man. The fisherman is never heavy. He is mostly a withered little old madman, with black claws, dirty rags (which he never changes), unkempt hair and beard, and a "ratty" expression. We cannot say that we ever saw him catch a fish, or even get a bite, and we certainly never saw him offer any for sale.

He gets a dozen or so lines out into the stream, with the shore end fastened to pegs or roots on the bank, and passed over sticks about four feet high, stuck in the mud; on the top of these sticks he hangs bullock-bells, or substitutes—jam-tins with stones fastened inside to bits of string. Then he sits down and waits. If the cod pulls the line the bell rings.

The fisherman is a great authority on the river and fish, but has usually forgotten everything else, including his name. He chops firewood for the boats sometimes, but it isn't his profession—he's a fisherman. He is only sane on points concerning the river, though he has all the fisherman's eccentricities. Of course he is a liar.

When he gets his camp fixed on one bank it strikes him he ought to be over on the other, or at a place up round the bend, so he shifts. Then he reckons he was a fool for not stopping where he was before. He never dies. He never gets older, or drier, or more withered-looking, or dirtier, or loonier—because he can't. We cannot imagine him as ever having been a boy, or even a youth. We cannot even try to imagine him as a baby. He is an animated mummy, who used to fish on the Nile three thousand years ago, and catch nothing.

We forgot to mention that there are wonderfully few wrecks on the Darling. The river boats seldom go down—their hulls are not built that way—and if one did go down it wouldn't sink far. But, once down, a boat is scarcely ever raised again; because, you see, the mud silts up round it and over it, and glues it, as it were, to the bottom of the river. Then the forty-foot alligators—which come down with the "Queenslan' rains", we suppose—root in the mud and fill their bellies with sodden flour and drowned deck-hands.

They tried once to blow up a wreck with dynamite because it (the wreck) obstructed navigation; but they blew the bottom out of the river instead, and all the water went through. The Government have been boring for it ever since. I saw some of the bores myself—there is one at Coonamble.

There is a yarn along the Darling about a cute Yankee who was invited up to Bourke to report on a proposed scheme for locking the river. He arrived towards the end of a long and severe drought, and was met at the railway-station by a deputation of representative bushmen, who invited him, in the first place, to accompany them to the principal pub—which he did. He had been observed to study the scenery a good deal while coming up in the train, but kept his conclusions to himself. On the way to the pub he had a look at the town, and it was noticed that he tilted his hat forward very often, and scratched the back of his head a good deal, and pondered a lot; but he refrained from expressing an opinion—even when invited to do so. He guessed that his opinions wouldn't do much good, anyway, and he calculated that they would keep till he got back "over our way"—by which it was reckoned he meant the States.

When they asked him what he'd have, he said to Watty the publican:

"Wal, I reckon you can build me your national drink. I guess I'll try it."

A long colonial was drawn for him, and he tried it. He seemed rather startled at first, then he looked curiously at the half-empty glass, set it down very softly on the bar, and leaned against the same and fell into reverie; from which he roused himself after a while, with a sorrowful jerk of his head.

"Ah, well," he said. "Show me this river of yourn."

They led him to the Darling, and he had a look at it.

"Is this your river?" he asked.

"Yes," they replied, apprehensively.

He tilted his hat forward till the brim nearly touched his nose, scratched the back of his long neck, shut one eye, and looked at the river with the other. Then, after spitting half a pint of tobacco juice into the stream, he turned sadly on his heel and led the way back to the pub. He invited the boys to "pisen themselves"; after they were served he ordered out the longest tumbler on the premises, poured a drop into it from nearly every bottle on the shelf, added a lump of ice, and drank slowly and steadily.

Then he took pity on the impatient and anxious population, opened his mouth, and spake.

"Look here, fellows," he drawled, jerking his arm in the direction of the river, "I'll tell you what I'll dew. I'll bottle that damned river of yourn in twenty-four hours!"

Later on he mellowed a bit, under the influence of several drinks which were carefully and conscientiously built from plans and specifications supplied by himself, and then, among other things, he said:

"If that there river rises as high as you say it dew—and if this was the States—why, we'd have had the *Great Eastern* up here twenty years ago"—or words to that effect.

Then he added, reflectively:

"When I come over here I calculated that I was going to make things hum, but now I guess I'll have to change my prospectus. There's a lot of loose energy laying round over our way, but I guess that if I wanted to make things move in your country I'd have to bring over the entire American nation—also his wife and dawg. You've got the makings of a glorious nation over here, but you don't get up early enough!"

The only national work performed by the blacks is on the Darling. They threw a dam of rocks across the river—near Brewarrina, we think—to make a fish-trap. It's there yet. But God only knows where they got the stones from, or how they carried them, for there isn't a pebble within forty miles.

The Mystery of Dave Regan

"AND then there was Dave Regan," said the traveller. "Dave used to die oftener than any other bushman I knew. He was always being reported dead and turnin' up again. He seemed to like it—except once, when his brother drew his money and drank it all to drown his grief at what he called Dave's 'untimely end'. Well, Dave went up to Queensland once with cattle, and was away three years and reported dead, as usual. He was drowned in the Bogan this time while tryin' to swim his horse across a flood—and his sweetheart hurried up and got spliced to a worse man before Dave got back.

"Well, one day I was out in the bush lookin' for timber, when the biggest storm ever knowed in that place come on. There was hail in it, too, as big as bullets, and if I hadn't got behind a stump and crouched down in time I'd have been riddled like a—like a bushranger. As it was, I got soakin' wet. The storm was over in a few minutes, the water ran off down the gullies, and the sun come out and the scrub steamed—and stunk like a new pair of moleskin trousers. I went on along the track, and presently I seen a long, lanky chap get on to a long, lanky horse and ride out of a bush yard at the edge of a clearin'. I knowed it was Dave d'reckly I set eyes on him.

"Dave used to ride a tall, holler-backed thoroughbred with a body and limbs like a kangaroo-dog, and it would circle around you and sidle away as if it was frightened you was goin' to jab a knife into it.

"'Ello, Dave!' said I, as he came spurrin' up. 'How are yer?'

"'Ello, Jim!' says he. 'How are you?'

"'All right!' says I. 'How are yer gettin' on?'

"But before we could say any more that horse shied away and broke off through the scrub to the right. I waited, because I knowed Dave would come back again if I waited long enough; and in about ten minutes he came sidlin' in from the scrub to the left.

"'Oh, I'm all right,' says he, spurrin' up sideways. 'How are you?'

" 'Right!' says I. 'How's the old people?'

" 'Oh, I ain't been home yet,' says he, holdin' out his hand; but afore I could grip it the cussed horse sidled off to the south end of the clearin' and broke away again through the scrub.

"I heard Dave swearin' about the country for twenty minutes or so, and then he came spurrin' and cursin' in from the other end of the clearin'.

" 'Where have you been all this time?' I said, as the horse came curvin' up like a boomerang.

" 'Gulf country,' said Dave.

" 'That was a storm, Dave,' said I.

" 'My oath!' says Dave.

" 'Get caught in it?'

" 'Yes.'

" 'Got to shelter?'

" 'No.'

" 'But you're as dry's a bone, Dave!'

"Dave grinned. '——and——and——the——!' he yelled.

"He said that to the horse as it boomeranged off again and broke away through the scrub. I waited; but he didn't come back, and I reckoned he'd got so far away before he could pull up that he didn't think it worth while comin' back; so I went on. By and by I got thinkin'. Dave was as dry as a bone, and I knowed that he hadn't had time to get to shelter, for there wasn't a shed within twelve miles. He wasn't only dry, but his coat was creased and dusty too—same as if he'd been sleepin' in a holler log; and when I come to think of it, his face seemed thinner and whiter than it used ter, and so did his hands and wrists, which always stuck a long way out of his coat-sleeves; and there was blood on his face—but I thought he'd got scratched with a twig. (Dave used to wear a coat three or four sizes too small for him, with sleeves that didn't come much below his elbows and a tail that scarcely reached his waist behind.) And his hair seemed dark and lank, instead of bein' sandy and stickin' out like an old fibre brush, as it used ter. And then I thought his voice sounded different, too. And when I inquired next day there was no one heard of Dave, and the chaps reckoned I must have been drunk, or seen his ghost.

"It didn't seem all right at all—it worried me a lot. I couldn't make out how Dave kept dry; and the horse and saddle and saddle-cloth was wet. I told the chaps how he talked to me and what he

Two Horsemen Approaching a Hut in the Bush

said, and how he swore at the horse; but they only said it was Dave's ghost and nobody else's. I told 'em about him bein' dry as a bone after gettin' caught in that storm; but they only laughed and said it was a dry place where Dave went to. I talked and argued about it until the chaps began to tap their foreheads and wink—then I left off talking. But I didn't leave off thinkin'—I always hated a mystery. Even Dave's father told me that Dave couldn't be alive or else his ghost wouldn't be round—he said he knew Dave better than that. One or two fellers did turn up afterwards that had seen Dave about the time that I did—and then the chaps said they was sure that Dave was dead.

"But one fine day, as a lot of us chaps was playin' pitch and toss at the shanty, one of the fellers yelled out:

" 'By Gee! Here comes Dave Regan!'

"And I looked up and saw Dave himself, sidlin' out of a cloud of dust on a long, lanky horse. He rode into the stockyard, got down, hung his horse up to a post, put up the rails, and then come slopin' towards us with a half-acre grin on his face. Dave had long, thin bow-legs, and when he was on the ground he moved as if he was on roller-skates.

" ' 'El-lo, Dave!' says I. 'How are yer?'

" ' 'Ello, Jim! ' said he. 'How the blazes are you?'

" 'All right!' says I, shakin' hands. 'How are yer?'

" 'Oh, I'm all right!' he says. 'How are yer poppin' up?'

"Well, when we'd got all that settled, and the other chaps had asked how he was, he said: 'Ah, well! Let's have a drink.'

"And all the other chaps crawfished up and flung themselves round the corner and sidled into the bar after Dave. We had a lot of talk, and he told us that he'd been down before, but had gone away without seein' any of us, except me, because he'd suddenly heard of a mob of cattle at a station two hundred miles away; and after a while I took him aside and said:

" 'Look here, Dave? Do you remember the day I met you after the storm?'

"He scratched his head.

" 'Why, yes,' he says.

" 'Did you get under shelter that day?'

" 'Why—no.'

" 'Then how the blazes didn't yer get wet?'

"Dave grinned; then he says:

" 'Why, when I seen the storm coming I took off me clothes and stuck 'em in a holler log till the rain was over.

" 'Yes,' he says, after the other coves had done laughin', but before I'd done thinking; 'I kept my clothes dry and got a good refreshin' shower-bath into the bargain.'

"Then he scratched the back of his neck with his little finger, and dropped his jaw, and thought a bit; then he rubbed the top of his head and his shoulder, reflective-like, and then he said:

" 'But I didn't reckon for them there blanky hailstones.' "

The Hairy Man

As far back as I can remember, the yarn of the Hairy Man was told in the Blue Mountains district of New South Wales. It scared children coming home by bush tracks from school and boys out late after lost cows; and even grown bushmen, when going along a lonely track after sunset, would hold their backs hollow and whistle a tune when they suddenly heard a thud, thud of a kangaroo leaping off through the scrub. Other districts also had spooks and bogies—the escaped tiger; the ghost of the convict who had been done to death and buried in his irons; ghosts of men who had hanged themselves; the ghost of the hawker's wife whose husband had murdered her with a tomahawk in the lonely camp by the track; the ghost of the murdered bushman whose mate quietly stepped behind him as he sat reflecting over a pipe and broke in the back of his head with an axe, and afterwards burnt the body between two logs; ghosts of victims whose murders had been avenged and of undiscovered murders that had been done right enough—all sorts and conditions of ghosts, none of them cheerful, most of them grimly original and characteristic of the weirdly melancholy and aggressively lonely Australian bush. But the Hairy Man was permanent, and his country spread from the eastern slopes of the Great Dividing Range right out to the ends of the western spurs. He had been heard of and seen and described so often and by so many reliable liars that most people agreed that there must be something. The most popular and enduring theory was that he was a gorilla, or an orang-outang which had escaped from a menagerie long ago. He was also said to be a new kind of kangaroo, or the last of a species of Australian animals which hadn't been discovered yet. Anyway, in some places, he was regarded as a danger to children coming home from school, as were wild bullocks, snakes, and an occasional bushman in the d.t.'s. So now and then, when the yarn had a revival, search parties were organized, and went out with guns to find the Hairy Man, and to settle him and the question one way or the other. But they never found him.

Dave Regan, Jim Bently and Andy Page, bush mates, had taken a contract to clear and fence the ground for a new cemetery about three miles out of the thriving township of Mudgee-Budgee. Mudgee-Budgee had risen to the dignity of a three-pub town, and people were beginning to die. Up to now the casual and scarce corpses of Mudgee-Budgee or of Home Rule, a goldfield six miles to the west—the bushman who had been thrown from his horse or smashed against a tree while riding recklessly, as bushmen do, or the boozer who had died during a spree in hot weather—had to be taken to the cemetery belonging to the farming town of Buckaroo, about nine miles east of Mudgee-Budgee. This meant a nine-mile, or, in the case of Home Rule, a fifteen-mile drag, which was a long-drawn-out agony in blazing hot, dusty weather, or even in the rain when the roads were boggy. The Buckaroo undertaker could only be induced to bring his hearse out two miles along the road to meet the corpse, which was carried so far in a drag, spring-cart, or wagonette. This so detracted from the dignity of Mudgee-Budgee and Home Rule that they agreed to get a cemetery between them, and Dave Regan got the contract to prepare the ground for corpse planting.

Dave and his mates camped in an old deserted slab and bark hut which happened to stand on the ground. It was a lonely place, which stood in a dark stringybark bush, the nearest house being the hut of a timber-getter and his family, about two miles along the track on the Home Rule side.

It was the day after Anniversary Day. Dave and Jim were patriots, and therefore were feeling very repentant and shaky. They had spent the day at the Buckaroo races, half the night in Buckaroo, and the other half in Home Rule, where the early-closing law as regarded public-houses was not stringent. They had enjoyed a good time; had betted and shouted away all their cash, as well as an advance drawn on the contract, had run up scores at all the pubs, and had been in several rows, and at least three fights. They weren't sure with whom, that was the trouble, but had a drink-lurid recollection of having got off their horses several times on the way home to fight each other. They were too sick to eat or to smoke yet; so they sat outside the hut with their nerves all unstrung and their imaginations therefore particularly active. Under these conditions they so magnified the awful importance of the unknown and the nightmare portions of the prior night that they felt very dismal and hopeless indeed. Dave had a haunting idea, which grew at last to be a sickening conviction, that he had insulted and had wanted to fight the big squatter of the district, from whom he had the promise of a big fencing contract. Jim has a smothering recollection of a row with the leading Mudgee-Budgee storekeeper, who gave them credit. And so they swore off drink—they were going to chuck it for good. Each was firmly resolved this time. But they said nothing about it to each other. They had sworn off mutually so often that the thing had become boresome. But the worst of it was that they had broken the bottle with the morning reviver, and had nothing to straighten up on, and their nerves were not in a fit state to allow of their going to Mudgee-Budgee at the risk of hearing some new and awful truths of last night's doings, and they hadn't the courage to ask Andy to go. They were very contrite and gentle towards him with their "Yes, Andy," and "No, Andy," and "No thank you, Andy," when he fried chops and made coffee for them. The day before they had both sworn to him—solemnly, affectionately, and at last impatiently, and even angrily—that they wouldn't get drunk, that they wouldn't bet, that they wouldn't draw a penny on the contract, that they'd buy a week's provisions first thing, that they'd bring the things home with them on their horses, and that they'd come home early. And now—they'd spent his money as well as their own! Andy made no remarks and asked no questions when they woke at midday; and they took his silence in a chastened spirit.

Andy Page was a patriot and a democrat, too, the most earnest of the three; but he was as obstinately teetotal as he was honest and truthful. Dave was the head of the party, but Andy was the father. Andy had, on several occasions, gone into town with Dave and Jim on pay nights—to look after them, to fight for them if necessary, and to get them home, if possible, when they'd had enough. It was a thankless job, but Andy was loved by his mates, who nevertheless, when drunk, even wanted to fight him when he stood out against "one more drink for the last". He was as strong physically, as well as morally, as the two put together; and was respected even by the publican whom he abused for serving his mates when they'd had enough. But the last spree but one had disgusted Andy. He swore he'd never go into town with them again, and like most simple-minded, honest, good-natured fellows whose ideas come slowly, who are slow to arriving at decisions (and whose decisions are nearly invariably right), when he'd once made up his mind nothing short of a severe shock of earthquake could move him. So he stayed at home on Anniversary Day, and washed and mended his clothes.

Dave and Jim were still moping wretchedly about the hut when, towards the middle of the afternoon, an angel came along on horseback. It was Jack Jones from Mudgee-Budgee, a drinking mate of theirs, a bush-telegraph joker, and the ne'er-do-well of the district. He hung up his shy, spidery filly under a shed at the back of the hut.

"I thought you chaps would be feeling shaky," he said, "and I've been feeling as lonely and dismal as a bandicoot on a burnt ridge, so I thought I'd come out. I've brought a flask of whisky."

Never were two souls more grateful. Bush mateship is a grand thing, drunk or sober.

Andy promptly took charge of the whisky, and proceeded to dole out judicious doses at decent intervals.

Jack, who was a sandy-complexioned young fellow with the expression of a born humorist, had some news.

"You know Corny George?" They had heard of him. He was an old Cornishman who split shingles and palings in the Black Range, and lived alone in a hut in a dark gully under the shadow of Dead Man's Gap.

"He went in to Buckaroo to the police station yesterday," said Jack Jones, "in a very bad state. He swore he'd seen the Hairy Man."

"The watter?"

"Yes, the Hairy Man. He swore that the Hairy Man had come down to his hut the night before last, just after dark, and tried to break in. The Hairy Man stayed about the hut all night, trying to pull the slabs off the walls, and get the bark off the roof, and didn't go away till daylight. Corny says he fired at him two or three times, through the cracks, with his old shot-gun, but the Hairy Man didn't take any notice. The old chap was pretty shaky on it."

"Drink, I s'pose," grunted Andy contemptuously.

"No, it wasn't drink. They reckoned he'd been 'hatting' it too long. They've got him at the police station."

"What did he say the Hairy Man was like?" asked Jim Bently.

"Oh, the usual thing," said Jack. " 'Bout as tall as a man and twice as broad, arms nearly as long as himself, big wide mouth with grinning teeth—and covered all over with red hair."

"Why, that's just what my uncle said he was like!" exclaimed Andy Page, suddenly taking great interest in the conversation. He was passing in with some firewood to stick under a pot in which he was boiling a piece of salt-beef; but he stood stock-still and stared at Jim Bently, with the blank, breathless expression of a man who had just heard astounding news.

"Did your uncle see the Hairy Man, Andy?" inquired Dave Regan feebly. He felt too sick to take much interest.

"Yes," said Andy, staring at Jack with great earnestness. "Didn't I tell you? He was drivin' home up the pass to Dead Man's Gap, where he lived then, and he seen the Hairy Man, bundlin' off among the rocks."

Andy paused impressively, and stared at Jack.

"And what did your uncle do, Andy?" asked Jack, with a jerky little cough.

"He stood up in the cart and hammered into the horse, and galloped it all the way home, full-bat up to the door; then he jumped down, leaving the cart and horse standing there, and went in and lay down on the bed, and wouldn't speak to anybody for two hours."

"How long?" asked Jim, still feebly.

"Two hours," said Andy earnestly, as he went in with the firewood.

Jack Jones proposed "a bit of a stroll"; he said it would do them good. He felt an irresistible inclination to giggle, and wished to get out of the hearing of Andy, whom he respected. As they slouched along the track there was an incident, which proved the state of their nerves. A big brown snake whipped across the dusty path into a head of dead boughs. They stared at each other for a full minute, then Jack summoned courage to ask:

"Did you chaps see that snake?"

"Yes."

And so it was all right. Then they put a match to the boughs, and stood round with long sticks till the snake came out.

They went back to the hut, and managed a cup of coffee. Presently they got on to ghost and Hairy Man yarns again.

"That was God's truth," said Jack, "that yarn I told you about what happened to me going up Dead Man's Pass. It was just as I told you. I was driving slowly up in that little old spring-cart of mine, when something—I don't know what it was—made me look behind, and there was a woman walking along behind the cart with her hands on the tail-board. It was just above the spot where the hawker's wife was murdered. She was dressed in black, and had black hair, and her face was dead white. At first I thought that it was some woman who wanted a lift, or a chap in woman's clothes playing the ghost, so I pulled up. And when I looked round again she was gone. I thought she'd crouched under the cart, so I whipped up the horse and then looked round again, but there was nothing there. Then I reckon I drove home as fast as Andy's uncle did. You needn't believe me unless you like."

"Thunderstorm coming," said Dave, sniffing and looking round the corner to the east. "I thought this weather would bring something."

"My oath," said Jim, "a regular old-man storm, too."

The big, blue-black bank of storm cloud rose bodily from the east, and was right overhead and sweeping down the sunset in a very few minutes. Then the lightning blazed out, and swallowed up daylight as well as darkness. But it was not a rain storm—it was the biggest hail storm ever experienced in that district. Orchards and vineyards were stripped, and many were ruined. Some said there were stones as big as hen's eggs; some said the storm lasted over an hour, and some said more—but the time was probably half or three-quarters of an hour. Hail lay feet deep in the old diggers' holes for a fortnight after. The mates half expected the hail to come through the roof of the hut.

Just as the storm began to hold up a little, they heard a louder pattering outside, and a bang at the door. The door was of hardwood boards with wide cracks; Andy rose to open it, but squinted through a crack first. Then he snatched the big crowbar from the corner, dug the foot of it into the earth floor, and jammed the pointed head under a cross-piece of the door; he did the same with a smaller crowbar, and looked wildly round for more material for a barricade.

"What are you doing? Who is it, Andy?" wildly cried the others.

"It's the Hairy Man!" gasped Andy.

They quickly got to the door and squinted through the cracks. One squint was sufficient. It was the Hairy Man right enough. He was about as tall as an ordinary man, but seemed twice as broad across the shoulders. He had long arms, and was covered with hair, face and all. He had a big, ugly mouth, and wild, bloodshot eyes. So they helped Andy to barricade the door.

There was another bang at the door. A cart rattled past, a woman screamed, and the cart went on at an increased pace. There was a shot-gun hanging on the wall, loaded—Andy had left it loaded to save ammunition the last time he'd been out kangaroo shooting. Andy, like most slow-thinking men, often did desperate things in a crisis. He snatched down the gun, stepped back a pace or two, aimed at the door low down, and fired. He doesn't know why he aimed low down—except that it "was too much like shooting at a man". They heard a howl, and the thing, whatever it was, running off. Then they barricaded the door some more ere they scanned the door planking and found that about half the charge had gone through.

"The powder must have got damp," said Andy. "I'll put in a double charge to make sure," and he re-loaded the gun with trembling hands.

The other three bumped their heads over the whisky. They can't say for certain how they got through that night or what they said or did. The first idea was to get out of there and run to Mudgee-Budgee, but they were reluctant to leave their fort. "Who'd go out and reconnoitre?" "Besides," said Jack Jones, "we're safer here, and the thing's gone, whatever it was. What would they think of us if we went into town with a yarn about a Hairy Man?" He had heard his horse breaking away, and didn't care to take the chance of being chased on foot.

About an hour later they heard a horse galloping past, and, looking through the cracks, saw a boy riding towards Mudgee-Budgee.

"It's young Foley," said Jack, "the son of that old timber-getter that's just taken up a selection along the road near Home Rule."

"I wonder what's up?" said Andy. "Perhaps the Hairy Man's been there. We ought to go along and help."

"They can take care of themselves," said Jack hurriedly. "They're close to Home Rule, and can get plenty of help. The boy wouldn't ride to Mudgee-Budgee if there was anything wrong."

The moon had risen full. Some two or three hours later they saw Mahoney, the mounted constable, and the young doctor from Buckaroo, ride past towards Home Rule.

"There's something up, right enough," said Jim Bently.

Later on, about daybreak, Andy was sitting obstinately on guard, with the gun across his knees and the others dozing on the bunks (and waking now and then with jerks), when Constable Mahoney rode up to the door and knocked a business knock that brought them all to their feet.

Andy asked him to come in, and placed a stool for him, but he didn't see it. He looked round the hut.

"Whose fowlin' piece is that?" he asked.

"It's—it's mine," said Andy.

Mahoney took the gun up and examined it.

"Is this fowlin' piece loaded?" he asked.

"Yes," said Andy, "it is."

"Now listen to me, boys," said the constable. "Was the fowlin' piece discharged last night?"

"Yes," said Andy, "it was."

"What's up? What have we done?" asked Jim Bently, desperately.

"Done?" shouted Mahoney. "Done? Why, you've filled old Foley's legs with kangaroo-shot. That's what you've done! Do you know what that is?"

"No," said Jack Jones. He was thinking hard.

"It's manslaughter!" roared Mahoney. "That's the meanin' of it!"

They explained what had happened as far as they were able. Now, Mahoney had a weakness for the boys, and a keen sense of humour—outside himself.

"Best come along with me," he said.

Andy had a stiff Sunday sac suit, of chocolate colour, and a starched white shirt and collar, which he kept in a gin case. He always put them all on when anything happened. On this occasion he fastened his braces over his waistcoat, and didn't notice it until he had gone some distance along the road.

There was great excitement at Foley's shanty—women and children crying, and neighbours hanging round.

Foley was lying on his face on a stretcher, while the young doctor was taking shot from the hairiest leg that Regan and Co. had ever seen on man or beast. The doctor said afterwards that some of the shot had only flattened inside the outer skin, and that others had a covering of hair twisted round them. When Foley was turned round to give his "dispositions", as Mahoney called them, they saw that he had enough hair on his chest to stuff a set of buggy cushions. He had red whiskers all over his face, rusty-red, spiky hair all over his head, and a big mouth and bloodshot eyes. He was the hairiest and ugliest man in the district.

His language was hardly understandable, partly because of the excitement he was still labouring under, and partly because of his peculiar shade of brogue. Where Mahoney said "shtone" Foley would say "stawn"—a brogue with a drawl which sounded ridiculous in an angry man. He drawled most over his oaths.

It seems that he was splitting fencing timber down "beyant the new cimitry", when the storm came on. He thought it would be the usual warm thunderstorm, and it was too far to run home. He didn't want to get wet, so he took his clothes off, and put them in a hollow log till the storm should be past. Then the lightning played round his tools—the cross-cut saw, axe, wedges, etc.—and he had to get away from there. He didn't bargain for "thim blanky hail-sta-w-ns". "It's a wonder I wasn't scalped and drilled full of hawls." He thought of the hut, and made for it, but they wouldn't let him in. Then he suddenly saw some women in a tilt cart comin' round a bend in the road, and saw no chance of getting out of sight— there was a clearing round the hut, so he banged at the door again. "I thawt the wimmin would stop."

"Whoy did ye think that?" asked Mahoney. "What would they shtop for?"

"How th' hell was I to know?—curiosity, I suppose. They welted into their old hawse, an', as I turned to look after thim, the murderin' villains inside shot a gun at me. I got back to me clawthes, an' dressed somehow. Someone will have to pay for it. I'll be laid up on me back for six weeks."

The young doctor excused himself, and went out for a few minutes. Mahoney winked at Regan and party—a wink you could hear —and it comforted them mightily. When they went out they saw the doctor hanging to a sapling, some distance from the hut. He swung with his back to the sapling, and slid to the ground, his legs stretched out in front of him. He said he would be all right presently.

The thing was fixed up, but the young doctor wanted badly to have the case brought into court. He said it would cheer up the district for years, and add ten years to the life of the oldest inhabitant.

On the Tucker Track

A STEELMAN STORY

STEELMAN and Smith, professional wanderers from New Zealand, took a run over to Australia one year to have a look at the country, and drifted outback, and played cards and "headin'-'em" at the shearing-sheds (while pretending to be strangers to each other), and sold eye-water and unpatented medicine, and worked the tucker tracks. They struck a streak of bad luck at West-o'-Sunday Station, where they were advised (by the boss and about fifty excited shearers) to go east, and not to stop till they reached the coast. They were tramping along the track towards Bourke; they were very hard up and had to battle for tucker and tobacco along the track. They came to a lonely shanty, about two camps west of Bourke.

"We'll turn off into the scrub and strike the track the other side of the shanty and come back to it," said Steelman. "You see, if they see us coming into Bourke they'll say to themselves, 'Oh, we're never likely to see these chaps again,' and they won't give us anything, or, perhaps, only a pinch of tea or sugar in a big lump of paper. There's some women that can never see a tucker-bag, even if you hold it right under their noses. But if they see us going outback they'll reckon that we'll get a shed likely as not, and we'll be sure to call there with our cheques coming back. I hope the old man's got the lumbago, or sciatica, or something."

"Why?" asked Smith.

"Because whenever I see an old man poking round the place on a stick I always make for him straight and inquire about his trouble; and no matter what complaint he's got, my old man suffered from it for years. It's pretty hard graft listening to an old man with a pet leg, but I find it pays; and I always finish up by advising him to try St Jacob's oil. Perhaps he's been trying it for years, but that doesn't matter; the consultation works out all right all the same, and there's never been a remedy tried yet but I've got another.

"I've got a lot of Maori and blackfellow remedies in my mind, and when they fail I can fall back on the Chinese; and if that isn't enough I've got a list of my grandmother's remedies that she wrote down for me when I was leaving home, and I kept it for a curiosity. It took her three days to write them, and I reckon they'll fill the bill.

"You don't want a shave. You look better with that stubble on. You needn't say anything; just stand by and wear your usual expression, and if they ask me what's the matter with my mate I'll fix up a disease for you to have, and get something extra on your account, poor beggar!

"I wish we had a chap with us that could sing a bit and run the gamut on a fiddle or something. With a sickly-looking fish like you to stand by and look interesting and die slowly of consumption all the time, and me to do the talking, we'd be able to travel from one end of the bush to the other and live on the fat of the land. I wouldn't cure you for a hundred pounds."

They reached the shanty, and there, sure enough, was an old man pottering round with a list to starboard. He was working with a hoe inside a low paling fence round a sort of garden. Steelman and Smith stopped outside the fence.

"Good day, boss!"

" 'Day."

"It's hot."

"It's hot."

So far it was satisfactory.

He was a little man, with a wiry, red beard. He might have been a Scandinavian.

"You seem to be a bit lame," said Steelman. "Hurt your foot?"

"Naw," said the old man. "It's an old thing."

"Ah!" said Steelman, "lumbago, I suppose? My father suffered cruel from it for years."

"Naw," said the old man, moving closer to the fence. "It ain't in me back; the trouble's with me leg."

"Oh!" said Steelman. "One a bit shorter than the other?"

"Well, yes. It seems to be wearin' a bit shorter. I must see to it."

"Hip disease, perhaps?" said Steelman. "A brother o' mine had——"

"Naw, it's not in the hip," said the old man. "My leg's gone at the knee."

"Oh, stiff joint; I know what that is. Had a touch of it once

119

myself. An uncle of mine was nearly crippled with it. He used to use St Jacob's oil. Ever try St Jacob's oil?"

"Naw," said the old man, "not that I know of. I've used linseed oil though."

"Linseed oil!" said Steelman; "I've never heard of that for stiff knee. How do you use it?"

"Use it raw," said the old man. "Raw linseed oil; I've rubbed it in, and I've soaked me leg in it."

"Soaked your leg in it!" said Steelman. "And did it do it any good?"

"Well, it seems to preserve it—keeps it from warping, and it wears better—and it makes it heavier. It seemed a bit too light before."

Steelman nudged Smith under cover of the palings. The old man was evidently a bit ratty.

"Well, I hope your leg will soon be all right, boss," said Steelman.

"Thank you," said the old man, "but I don't think there's much hope. I suppose you want some tucker?"

"Well, yes," said Steelman, rather taken aback by the old man's sudden way of putting it. "We're hard up."

"Well, come along to the house and I'll see if I can get yer something," said the old man; and they walked along outside the fence, and he hobbled along inside, till he came to a little gate at the corner. He opened the gate and stumped out. He had a wooden leg. He wore his trouser-leg down over it, and the palings had hidden the bottom from Steelman and Smith.

He wanted them to stay to dinner, but Steelman didn't feel comfortable, and thanked him, and said they'd rather be getting on (Steelman always spoke for Smith); so the old man gave them some cooked meat, bread, and a supply of tea and sugar. Steelman watched his face very close, but he never moved a muscle. But when they looked back he was leaning on his hoe, and seemed to be shaking.

"Took you back a bit, Steely, didn't it!" suggested Smith.

"How do you make that out?" snorted Steelman, turning on him suddenly. "I knew a carpenter who used to soak his planes in raw linseed oil to preserve them and give them weight. There's nothing funny about that."

Smith rubbed his head.

King William

THERE was a blackfellow in Albany who used to make his rude weapons of wood and stone at a carpenter's bench, and with such tools as he could cadge or borrow—including files and grindstone. When the English or French mailboat was signalled he'd gather the remnants of his tribe and retire to the scrub to make-up—and, maybe, hold a dress rehearsal. Thusly, the first sight that greeted the wide eyes and open mouths of eager new-chums—come ashore for an hour's run, and racing up the jetty to see whose foot would be the first on Australian soil—would be a dusky warrior chief in all his native glory. A possum-rug on his shoulders, a fearsome and wonderful arrangement (that would have put any fashion of Paris hats in the shade) of sticks, reeds, grass, clay, and whitewash, on his head, and his noble, savage lineaments "picked out" to an alarming extent with whiting and red raddle and ochre (cadged from one of the house-painters). Standing erect, motionless and silent, seemingly impassive as the Sphinx; boomerang, stone tomahawk, etc., in left hand; spear (grounded) in right; and the remnant of his tribe ("Mrs Williams" —ugliest gin in the known West; Old Sally, and Dirty Dick) grouped at his feet.

Describe a circle of newchums and tourists—some dressed in the latest London fashion; the majority with open eyes, and mouths and ears stretched to the limit, and awe, or respect, if anything, in their expressions—and one or two saloon passengers, or "jokers", who saw through the thing at the first glance, and are enjoying the show from behind, as well as in front, and willing to pay for the extra fun—all of which noted by and well known to William Rex, who, if the spirit moved him, and he thought it safe and judicious, from a business point of view, would acknowledge or recognize the superior intelligence of the aforesaid keen observers amongst his possible patrons by solemnly, slowly, yet momentarily closing down the whitewashed lid of the awful bloodshot optic that was on their side. That wink "doubled-up" many an observant humorist—to the surprise of more sober fellow-passengers, who couldn't see what there was to laugh at.

The gins offered rugs and weapons for sale with one hand—holding the other, all the time, rigidly extended, the wrist resting on a drawn-up knee; never for a moment drawing in the black and yellow begging claw—and they, or Dirty Dick—or, perchance, a hireling half-caste (in the character of a slave), if such suited the passengers' fancies, or imaginations—answered questions and interpreted when absolutely necessary from a business point of view. It was understood, or supposed to be understood, to be beneath the dignity of the dusky chief to hold converse directly with the pale-faced strangers, whose fathers had slain his warriors, and laid waste his hunting-grounds.

To the white natives the scene was commonplace, of course, and passed unnoticed, and unchuckled at; but the elaborate simplicity of it all was very restful and comforting to me. Billy himself could see and enjoy the humour of it—after he had carefully secured the "gate" from the gins; otherwise, he regarded the whole thing from a strictly business point of view, as hinted above. There seems sometimes a touch of Scotch in King Billy. I was his first victim, but later on, when I got to know him—and he me—he said he'd get me a genuine stone tomahawk, such as the blacks used, by means of a blackfellow who was going north-west to join a party of blacks, who were in touch with a tribe of the interior—so I shouted for him now and then. But—well, I left before the weapon had time to be passed south, and so I remain undecided as to whether there is or is not a touch of Irish in King William, also.

I have invented—or altered—the names for the Last of Their Race. Mrs Williams may be living yet—and she made determined attempts to get out a summons for "dafamation" of character against a friend of mine, who, innocently, and at the suggestion of a better-informed, but totally unprincipled, brother humorist, addressed her as "Miss" Williams. She subsequently tried to settle the matter out of court, too, with a billet of hardwood. Take the ugliest Chinaman (and there are some fairly plain ones) in Lower George Street, give him a coat of lampblack mixed with turpentine—or black lead (never mind the polish)—and you'll have a fair idea of Mrs Williams, who was so enthusiastic concerning her fair fame. But, there, I'm not trying to score a point at the expense of my black countrymen. This "Ad.", if I know anything of human nature

The Newly Arrived
Dixson Galleries, State Library of New South Wales

—and King Billy still runs his little "silver coin" show—will bring him extra sixpences, and good luck to him!—the lowest and most degraded, most cheerful, humorous, and by me at least, and least of his subjects, most kindly-thought-of of monarchs.

We Called Him "Ally" for Short

I DON'T believe in ghosts; I never did have any sympathy with them, being inclined to regard them as a nuisance and a bore. A ghost generally comes fooling around when you want to go to sleep, and his conversation, if he speaks at all, invariably turns on murders and suicides and other unpleasant things in which you are not interested, and which only disturb your rest. It is no use locking the door against a ghost, for, as is well known, he can come in through the keyhole, and there are cases on record when a ghost has been known to penetrate a solid wall. You cannot kick a ghost out; he is impervious to abuse; and if you throw a boot at him, likely as not it will go right through a new looking-glass worth eighteen shillings.

I remember, about five years ago, I was greatly annoyed by a ghost, while doing a job of fencing in the bush between here and Perth. I was camping in an old house which had been used as a barrack for the convicts or their keepers (I'm not sure which) in the lively old days of the broad arrow. He was a common-looking ghost of a skeleton kind, and was arrayed in what appeared to be the tattered remnants of an old-time convict uniform. He still wore a pair of shadowy manacles, but, being very elastic and unsubstantial and stretching the full length of his stride, he did not seem to notice them at all. He had a kind of Artful Dodger expression about his bare jaw-bones, and in place of the ordinary halo of the ring variety he wore a shining representation of a broad arrow which shed a radiance over his skull. He used to come round and wake me about midnight with a confounded rigmarole about a convict who was buried alive in his irons, and whose representative my unwelcome visitor claimed to be. I tried all I knew to discourage him. I told him I wasn't interested and wanted to go to sleep; but his perseverance wore me out at last, and I tried another tack. I listened to his confounded yarn from beginning to end, and sympathized with him, and told him that he, or the individual he represented, had been treated confoundedly badly; and I promised to make a poem about it.

But even then he wasn't satisfied. Nothing would suit him but he must spin his old yarn, and be sympathized with about seven times a week, always choosing the most unbusinesslike hours (between one and three in the morning) for his disclosures. At last I could stand it no longer. I was getting thin and exhausted from want of sleep, so I determined on a course of action. I had a dog at home, a big black dog with unpleasant eyes, and a chewing-up apparatus that an alligator might have envied. He had a most enterprising appetite, and wasn't. afraid of anything on the surface of this earth—or under it, as far as he could burrow. He would gnaw a log to pieces rather than let the possum it contained escape him. He was not the sort of dog to stand any nonsense even from a ghost. His full name was Alligator-Desolation (we called him Ally for short): and, as I considered that if any person on earth could lay the ghost that annoyed me that person was Alligator-Desolation, I declared to bring him.

The next time I journeyed home for rations I brought Alligator-Desolation back with me. On the trip back he killed 5 kangaroos, 16 possums, 4 native rats, 2 native bears, 3 sheep, a cow and a calf, and another dog that happened by; and before he had been two hours at the hut he had collected enough carcasses of indigenous animals to stink a troop out in a week, or to feed all the dogs in Constantinople.

I had tea and a smoke while Ally was resting, and about 11 o'clock I lay down in my bunk, dressed as I was, and waited. At about one I heard the usual unearthly noises which accompanied the arrival of my friend the ghost, and Ally went out to investigate. While the dog was gone, the ghost strolled in through the door of the end room, apparently unconscious of his danger. He glided straight up to the side of my bunk, took his accustomed seat on a gin-case, and commenced in a doleful voice to pitch his confounded old yarn again; but he hadn't uttered half a dozen ghostly words when Alligator-Desolation came in through the side door.

The ghost caught sight of Ally before the latter saw him, and made for the window. Ally wasn't far behind; he made a grab at the ghost's nether garments, but they gave way easily, being of a ghostly material. Then Ally leapt out through the window and chased the ghost three times round the house, and then the latter came in through an opening in the wall where a slab had fallen out. Being of an easily compressible constitution he came through, of course, with the facility peculiar to his kind, but the crack was narrow and the dog stuck fast. His ghostship made the best of his opportunity, and, approaching my bed, hurriedly endeavoured to continue his story, as though his ghostly existence depended on it. But his utterances were drowned by the language of Alligator, whose canine oaths were simply terrific. At last, collecting all his energy for one mighty effort, Alligator came through, bringing down the slabs on each side of him.

He made for the ghost at once, and the ghost made for the window. This time Alligator made a grab for the spectre's ankle, and his teeth came together with a crash that threatened their destruction. Ally must have been greatly astonished and disgusted, because he so seldom missed anything he reached for. But he wasn't the kind of dog to give up. He leapt through the window, and, after a race round the hut, lasting some minutes, the ghost gave it up, and made for the scrub. Seeing the retreat through a crack in the slabs, I immediately rose, went outside and mounted my horse, which I had kept ready saddled in case of emergency. I followed the chase for about five miles, and at last reached a mound under some trees, which looked like an old grave. Down through this mound the ghost dived.

Alligator-Desolation immediately commenced to dig, and made two feet in no time. It appeared that a wombat had selected the grave as a suitable site for the opening of his burrow and, after having sunk about three feet, was resting from his labours. There was a short and angry interview between Alligator and the wombat, during which the latter expired, and then Ally continued his work of excavation. After sinking two feet deeper he dragged out what appeared to be the leg-bone of a human being, attached to which was a pair of heavy leg-irons, such as were used in the old convict days. Ally went down the hole again, but presently he paused in his digging operations, and I heard a noise like a row in the infernal regions. Then a thin, shadowy form issued from the grave and made off through the scrub with the dog in pursuit.

My horse was knocked up, so I left the chase to Alligator and returned home to await developments. Ally came back about three days later with his hair badly singed and smelling strongly of brimstone. I have no doubt that he chased the ghost to the infernal regions and perhaps had an interview with Cerberus at the gate, or the boss himself; but the dog's tail was well up and a satisfied grin oozed from the roots of every fang, and by the same tokens I concluded that the other party, whoever he was, had got left.

I haven't seen the ghost since.

Taking Stiffner Down

THERE were three of us, travelling in the interests of three or more city firms, and doing our best to make expenses, salaries and commissions by persuading Jim and Bill & Co. that we were travelling solely in their interests at great personal sacrifice and inconvenience.

We were following the shows—after the manner of one-horse circuses, dramatic and variety companies, phonograph, etc., three-card, try-your-anything, pill-and-tooth-powder and novelty and racing men, and the rest of the army of hardworking spielers. Country shows are got up and run mainly in the interests of these and of the local publican, politician and storekeeper. The prize bull, square cart-horse, big pumpkins, swelled hogs, and their producer and owner—the Specimen Flat—are only tolerated as an excuse for the rest.

We had hired a trap to take us from the railway terminus at Dead Camel to a show at Starving Steers—a township consisting mostly of a pub and outhouses. We were pressed for time. We should have been in the previous day in order to commence cultivating the interests of Jim and Bill—the night before the show opened—by making them drunk at their own expense, and drawing them out with a view of ascertaining their longfelt wants and supplying them by order. They seldom wanted much drawing out —God bless 'em. We'll cure the bush of its simple faith and good-nature in time.

The road to Starving Steers was mostly travelled in the interests of one Stiffner, of the Not There Hotel—a half-way house. It was a rough bush track through flat scrub country. Stiffner was a rough case with a hard reputation. Our trip had been dull so far.

"I knew this Stiffner in New Zealand," said Spooner, who travelled for Fleece and Bellywool. "We'll take a rise out of him."

Porter and I agreed. Porter was travelling for Cole Tee & Co., the wine merchants, and I was with him part of this trip.

The usual outback shanty. Stiffner was a big, rough man with a black, burly look, and his voice sounded so.

"Good day!"

" 'Day," grunted Stiffner.

We got down and stretched. I looked him over and decided to take mine without any Stiffner in it; but Spooner was plucky—or mostly knew his man and acted on his instinct, which amounts to the same thing as pluck. He walked up to Stiffner, nudged him and said:

"Jus' look in my ear, will yeh?"

"What!" snorted Stiffner.

"Jus' look in my ear, will yeh?" repeated Spooner, taking the lobe of his ear between his finger and thumb and jerking it out towards Stiffner.

Stiffner thought a moment and scowled, then he said:

"Ask the man with the specs."

Spooner looked round. Of course there was no man with spectacles.

"I'll have you yet," said Spooner.

"You can't," said Stiffner, wearily. "We've got too much time to think out here."

That was the end of the first round. We picked Spooner up, so to speak, and rubbed him down the wrong way. Then I said:

"Ah, well, have you got anything to drink?"

"Yes," said Stiffner. "Whisky, rum, and brandy—and gin. Sling out the dollar."

I threw two florins on the bar, Stiffner swept them into the till and served us.

"Well, where's my change?" I asked.

"What change?"

"I want a bob back out of that—there's only three drinks at a bob a drink."

"I think there's four," said Stiffner, reaching for a special bottle.

"How the devil do you make that out?"

Stiffner poured out a nip for himself, said "Here's luck!" and tossed it off. It was just as Stiffner thought.

"Bill," he shouted, to one of the men hanging about, "get some water into the trough for those horses—will yer?"

That was the second round. Spooner got back on me.

We hung about the veranda and thought mostly. Stiffner came out and leaned his elbow against the veranda-post and regarded the horses in an abstracted manner.

We went in again and Porter shouted. He put three shillings down.

Stiffner said, "Thank you. You'd better have a drop of this, it's the last I got left," and he gave Porter a nip out of his own special bottle.

So Porter's try was a failure. It looked mean. Porter was impulsive and sensitive, so he flung out half-a-crown and asked Stiffner to have another drink with us. There were a couple of swagmen in the bar, and Porter invited them to join, in case the three-shilling business might have looked mean to them.

Third round. We felt very much towards Porter as Napoleon did towards Soult when the Prussians turned up where they weren't wanted at Waterloo.

I heard that Stiffner had some sheep, and a thought struck me. I nudged Spooner, and said to Stiffner:

"By the way, you've got some sheep. My friend here is something in your line. You might do some business with him."

"How's that?" he asked suspiciously.

"Oh, no funny business. This is Mr Spooner—Fleece and Belly-wool's man. You might arrange with him about your clip. Show the boss your card, Spooner."

Stiffner looked a little more civil—scented business perhaps. He took the card and read it.

"Well, Mr Spooner," he said, shaking hands, "I'm glad to meet you. What can I do for you?"

"Read the other side of the card," said Spooner.

Stiffner turned it over and read in pencil the words: "Stiffner you ——— your pants are all torn behind."

Stiffner clapped his hands to the seat of his britches with an oath, but they were all right, of course.

"I'll have you yet!"

He shouted.

This was the fourth round. Perhaps the Prussians weren't coming, after all.

We got into the buggy. There were two tracks branching away from the corner of the pub and one seemed as likely as the other.

"Which is our track?" we asked.

"Dunno," said Stiffner. "I couldn't give it away. Better toss up for it—heads for the right, tails for the left. . . . Heads it is."

"Oh, come now!" I said. "Let up on it. A joke's a joke."

"So it is," agreed Stiffner. "It's all right, chaps; any track will do. There's no difference—they both go the same way."

So we drove off on the right-hand track. We were used to the eccentricities of bush tracks.

"See you agen," he shouted after us.

"Right you are, old man. Good-bye!"

After driving for an hour or so through the eternal sameness of the scrub, we brought up at the corner of Stiffner's stable.

That track went round in a circle through the scrub and came back to the starting place. Stiffner had either traced it purposely with his cart wheels or had been in the habit of going out one way for wood or water and coming round home the other way. Perhaps the tracks were accidental, but we doubted it.

Stiffner was leaning on a panel by the trough with his elbow on the rail and his chin in his hands.

"I've mended them pants," he observed quietly, without moving. We caved in.

He said it was our shout, and so it was. He charged us five shillings for horse-feed, and when we were ready to go he showed us the right track, which started through the scrub from the back door of the kitchen.

"So long, chaps," said Stiffner. "You'll find a bottle in the back of the buggy."

"Good-bye, Stiffner," we said. "We'll see you again."

"Don't think you will," he said wearily. Then he added in a sad, tired kind of voice: "We've got too blessed much time to think out here."

And we drove off into the sad Australian sunset.

The Chinaman's Ghost

"SIMPLE as striking matches," said Dave Regan, bushman; "but it gave me the biggest scare I ever had—except, perhaps, the time I stumbled in the dark into a six-foot digger's hole, which might have been eighty feet deep for all I knew when I was falling. (There was an eighty-foot shaft left open close by.)

"It was the night of the day after the Queen's birthday. I was sinking a shaft with Jim Bently and Andy Page on the old Redclay goldfield, and we camped in a tent on the creek. Jim and me went to some races that was held at Peter Anderson's pub, about four miles across the ridges, on Queen's birthday. Andy was a quiet sort of chap, a teetotaller, and we'd disgusted him the last time he was out for a holiday with us, so he stayed at home and washed and mended his clothes, and read an arithmetic book. (He used to keep the accounts, and it took him most of his spare time.)

"Jim and me had a pretty high time. We all got pretty tight after the races, and I wanted to fight Jim, or Jim wanted to fight me—I don't remember which. We were old chums, and we nearly always wanted to fight each other when we got a bit on, and we'd fight if we weren't stopped. I remember once Jim got maudlin drunk and begged and prayed of me to fight him, as if he was praying for his life. Tom Tarrant, the coach-driver, used to say that Jim and me must be related, else we wouldn't hate each other so much when we were tight and truthful.

"Anyway, this day, Jim got the sulks, and caught his horse and went home early in the evening. My dog went home with him, too; I must have been carrying on pretty bad to disgust the dog.

"Next evening I got disgusted with myself, and started to walk home. I'd lost my hat, so Peter Anderson lent me an old one of his, that he'd worn on Ballarat he said: it was a hard, straw, flat, broad-brimmed affair, and fitted my headache pretty right. Peter gave me a small flask of whisky to help me home. I had to go across some flats and up a long dark gully called Murderer's Gully, and over a gap called Dead Man's Gap, and down the ridge and gullies of Redclay Creek. The lonely flats were covered with blue-grey gum-bush, and looked ghostly enough in the moonlight, and I was pretty shaky, but I had a pull at the flask and a mouthful of water at a creek and felt right enough. I began to whistle and then to sing: I never used to sing unless I thought I was a couple of miles out of earshot of anyone.

"Murderer's Gully was deep and pretty dark most times, and of course it was haunted. Women and children wouldn't go through it after dark; and even me, when I'd grown up, I'd hold my back pretty holler, and whistle, and walk quick going along there at night-time. We're all afraid of ghosts, but we won't let on.

"Someone had skinned a dead calf during the day and left it on the track, and it gave me a jump, I promise you. It looked like two corpses laid out naked. I finished the whisky and started up over the gap. All of a sudden a great old-man kangaroo went across the track with a thud-thud, and up the sidling, and that startled me. Then the naked, white, glistening trunk of a stringybark tree, where someone had stripped off a sheet of bark, started out from a bend in the track in a shaft of moonlight, and that gave me a jerk. I was pretty shaky before I started. There was a Chinaman's grave close by the track on the top of the gap. An old Chow had lived in a hut there for many years, and fossicked on the old diggings, and one day he was found dead in the hut, and the Government gave someone a pound to bury him. When I was a nipper we reckoned that his ghost haunted the gap, and cursed in Chinese because the bones hadn't been sent home to China. It was a lonely, ghostly place enough.

"It had been a smotheringly hot day and very close coming across the flats and up the gully—not a breath of air; but now as I got higher I saw signs of the thunderstorm we'd expected all day, and felt the breath of a warm breeze on my face. When I got into the top of the gap the first thing I saw was something white amongst the dark bushes over the spot where the Chinaman's grave was, and I stood staring at it with both eyes. It moved out of the shadow presently, and I saw that it was a white bullock, and I felt relieved. I'd hardly felt relieved when, all at once, there came a 'pat-pat-pat' of running feet close behind me! I jumped round quick, but there was nothing there, and while I stood staring all ways for Sunday there came a 'pat-pat', then a pause, and then 'pat-pat-pat-pat' behind me again: it was like someone dodging and running off that time. I started to walk down the track pretty fast, but hadn't gone a dozen yards when, 'pat-pat-pat', it was close behind me again. I jerked my eyes over my shoulder but kept my legs going. There was nothing behind, but I fancied I saw something slip into the bush to the right. It must have been the moonlight on the moving boughs; there was a good breeze blowing now. I got down to a more level track, and was making across a spur to the main road when 'Pat-pat, pat-pat-pat, pat-pat-pat!' it was after me again. Then I began to run—and it began to run, too! 'pat-pat-pat' after me all the time. I hadn't time to look round. Over the spur and down the sidling and across the flat to the road I went as fast as I could split my legs apart. I had a scared idea that I was getting a touch of the jim-jams, and that frightened me more than any outside ghost could have done. I stumbled a few times, and saved myself, but just before I reached the road I fell slithering on to my hands on the grass and gravel. I thought I'd broken both my wrists. I stayed for a moment on my hands and knees, quaking and listening, squinting round like a great goanna; I couldn't hear nor see anything. I picked myself up, and had hardly got on one end when, 'pat-pat!' it was after me again. I must have run a mile and a half altogether that night. It was still about three-quarters of a mile to the camp, and I ran till my heart beat in my head and my lungs choked up in my throat. I saw our tent-fire and took off my hat to run faster. The footsteps stopped, then something about the hat touched my fingers, and I stared at it—and the thing dawned on me. I hadn't noticed at Peter Anderson's—my head was too swimmy to notice anything. It was an old hat of the style that the first diggers used to wear, with a couple of loose ribbon ends, three or four inches long, from the band behind. As long as I walked quietly through the gully, and there was no wind, the tails didn't flap, but when I got up into the breeze they flapped or were still according to how the wind lifted them or pressed them down flat on the brim. And when I ran they tapped all the time; and the hat being tight on my head, the tapping of the ribbon ends against the straw sounded loud, of course.

"I sat down on a log for a while to get some of my wind back and cool down, and then I went to the camp as quietly as I could, and had a long drink of water.

"'You seem to be a bit winded, Dave,' said Jim Bently, 'and mighty thirsty. Did the Chinaman's ghost chase you?'

"I told him not to talk rot, and went into the tent, and lay down on my bunk, and had a good rest."

Leggo Me Ear

UNCLE Abel was a silent man who seldom said the same thing twice to the same person. He would say a thing and have done with it. And he was never known to speak ill of any member of the family. If one started to do it about another to Uncle Abel, Uncle Abel would listen until he saw the drift, and then say decisively and finally:

"Leggo me ear!"

That usually concluded the interview.

He'd stand a bore as long as ever he could, and at last say:

"*For the Lord's sake*, leggo me ear!"

He would listen to commercial travellers, canvassers, blokes, fellows, chaps, coves who wanted to put him on to a good thing, and confidence men and spielers of all descriptions, until they seemed to have amused themselves sufficiently, and then he'd say laconically:

"Leggo me ear."

It was very disconcerting, especially to confidence men, spielers, and fly young blokes.

After his wife, Aunt Anne, had nagged him for an hour or so—and she was the champion nagger of a large and discontented family—Uncle Abel would say warningly:

"Leggo me ear."

This would really start her. What came before had only been a prelude. Uncle Abel would stand it for half an hour or so, and then give her a last chance.

"For the love of heaven, woman, if you have any sense stop right there and leggo me ear!"

Uncle Abel very, very seldom swore, by the way, but when he did—! He'd stand her for another half-hour or so, or until his head swam and hummed, and he thought he was going off it. Then he'd spring to his feet, put his fist through a window, a picture, a looking-glass, his hat—or hers—or anything handy and suitable, and roar:

"You something something of a something of a woman!—*Leggo me flamin' hear!*"

Then she'd be satisfied, and go about her housework with a sweetly patient and resigned manner and expression for the rest of the morning.

With the co-operation of her sisters she managed to get Uncle Abel tidied up and into chapel one Sunday afternoon. It was hot and drowsy, the sermon was long, and the layman who "held service" that day was a dreary and conceited bore. Uncle Abel dozed, and being disturbed by extra loud ranting, and imperfectly conscious of his locality, he said sleepily, yet distinctly:

"Leggo me ear."

They steered him out, and the family said they'd never be able to hold up their heads in the district again for very shame. But they got over it in time. Uncle Abel's remark was popular with the young men—and old ones, too.

In dead earnest he upset an electioneering meeting with it once, and ruined the candidate's chances in that district for ever.

Aunt Anne drove him to beer, and a few years later he died of alcoholic poisoning aggravated by being thrown from his horse on a hard road on a hot day, and letting fourteen bullocks and a load of wool pass over him.

After the doctor, they brought the parson.

Uncle Abel was conscious, and the parson droned along in the usual way for some time. At last Uncle Abel seemed wishful to speak, muttered something painfully, and tried to rise.

"I cannot hear what you say, my brother," said the clergyman, bending down his ear; then, as Uncle Abel still strove to rise, "Wait, my poor brother, I will support your head," and he slipped an arm under Uncle Abel's neck. "Now, brother, speak!"

Uncle Abel gasped, "*Leggo me ear!*"

"What is that you said, brother?" asked the good man with intense anxiety.

"*Leggo me hear!*"

And he fell back.

Steelman's Pupil

STEELMAN was a hard case, but some said that Smith was harder. Steelman was big and good-looking, and good-natured in his way; he was a spieler, pure and simple, but did things in humorous style. Smith was small and weedy, of the sneak variety; he had a whining tone and a cringing manner. He seemed to be always so afraid you were going to hit him that he would make you *want* to hit him on that account alone.

Steelman "had" you in a fashion that would make your friends laugh. Smith would "have" you in a way which made you feel mad at the bare recollection of having been taken in by so contemptible a little sneak.

They battled round together in the North Island of Maoriland for a couple of years.

One day Steelman said to Smith:

"Look here, Smithy, you don't know you're born yet. I'm going to take you in hand and teach you."

And he did. If Smith wouldn't do as Steelman told him, or wasn't successful in cadging, or mugged any game they had in hand, Steelman would threaten to stoush him; and, if the warning proved ineffectual after the second or third time, he *would* stoush him.

One day, on the track, they came to a place where an old Scottish couple kept a general store and shanty. They camped alongside the road, and Smith was just starting up to the house to beg supplies when Steelman cried:

"Here!—hold on. Now where do you think you're going to?"

"Why, I'm going to try and chew the old party's lug, of course. We'll be out of tucker in a couple of days," said Smith.

Steelman sat down on a stump in a hopeless, discouraged sort of way.

"It's no use," he said, regarding Smith with mingled reproach and disgust. "It's no use. I might as well give it best. I can see that it's a waste of time trying to learn you anything. Will I ever be able to knock some gumption into your thick skull? After all the time

137

and trouble and pains I've took with your education, you hain't got any more sense than to go and mug a business like that! When will you learn sense? Hey? After all, I——Smith, you're a born mug!"

He always called Smith a "mug" when he was particularly wild at him, for it hurt Smith more than anything else.

"There's only two classes in the world, spielers and mugs—and you're a mug, Smith."

"What have I done, anyway?" asked Smith helplessly. "That's all I want to know."

Steelman wearily rested his brow on his hand.

"That will do, Smith," he said listlessly; "don't say another word, old man; it'll only make my head worse; don't talk. You might, at the very least, have a little consideration for my feelings—even if you haven't for your own interests." He paused and regarded Smith sadly. "Well, I'll give you another show. I'll stage the business for you."

He made Smith doff his coat and get into his worst pair of trousers—and they were bad enough; they were hopelessly "gone" beyond the extreme limit of bush decency. He made Smith put on a rag of a felt hat and a pair of 'lastic-sides which had fallen off a tramp and lain baking and rotting by turns on a rubbish-heap; they had to be tied on Smith with bits of rag and string. He drew dark shadows round Smith's eyes, and burning spots on his cheekbones with some grease-paints he used when they travelled as "The Great Steelman and Smith Combination Star Dramatic Co." He damped Smith's hair to make it dark and lank, and his face more corpse-like by comparison—in short, he made him up to look like a man who had long passed the very last stage of consumption, and had been artificially kept alive in the interests of science.

"Now, you're ready," said Steelman to Smith. "You left your whare the day before yesterday and started to walk to the hospital at Palmerston. An old mate picked you up dying on the road, brought you round, and carried you on his back most of the way here. You firmly believe that Providence had something to do with the sending of that old mate along at that time and place above all others. Your mate also was hard up; he was going to a job—the first show of work he'd had in nine months—but he gave it up to see you through; he'd give up his life rather than desert a mate in trouble. You only want a couple of shillings or a bit of tucker to

Satan Rebuking Sin
Dixson Galleries, State Library of New South Wales

help you on to Palmerston. You know you've got to die, and you only want to live long enough to get word to your poor old mother, and die on a bed.

"Remember, they're Scotch up at that house. You understand the Scotch barrack pretty well by now—if you don't it ain't my fault. You were born in Aberdeen, but came out too young to remember much about the town. Your father's dead. You ran away to sea and came out in the *Bobbie Burns* to Sydney. Your poor old mother's in Aberdeen now—Bruce or Wallace Wynd will do. Your mother might be dead now—poor old soul!—anyway, you'll never see her again. You wish you'd never run away from home. You wish you'd been a better son to your poor old mother; you wish you'd written to her and answered her last letter. You only want to live long enough to write home and ask for forgiveness and a blessing before you die. If you had a drop of spirits of some sort to brace you up you might get along the road better. (Put this delicately.) Get the whine out of your voice and breathe with a wheeze—like this; get up the nearest approach to a death-rattle that you can. Move as if you were badly hurt in your wind—like this. (If you don't do it better'n that, I'll stoush you.) Make your face a bit longer and keep your lips dry—don't lick them, you damned fool!—*breathe* on them; make 'em dry as chips. That's the only decent pair of breeks you've got, and the only shoon. You're a Presbyterian—not a U.P., the Auld Kirk. Your mate would have come up to the house only —well, you'll have to use the stuffing in your head a bit; you can't expect me to do all the brain work. Remember it's consumption you've got—galloping consumption; you know all the symptoms —pain on top of your right lung, bad cough, and night sweats. Something tells you that you won't see the new year—it's a week off Christmas now. And if you come back without anything, I'll blessed soon put you out of your misery."

Smith came back with about four pounds of shortbread and as much various tucker as they could conveniently carry; a pretty good suit of cast-off tweeds; a new pair of 'lastic-sides from the store stock; two bottles of patent medicine and a black bottle half-full of home-made consumption-cure; also a letter to a hospital-committee man and three shillings to help him on his way to Palmerston. He also got about half a mile of sympathy, religious consolation, and medical advice which he didn't remember.

"*Now*," he said triumphantly, "am I a mug or not?"

Steelman kindly ignored the question. "I *did* have a better opinion of the Scotch," he said, contemptuously.

Steelman got on at an hotel as billiard-marker and decoy, and in six months he managed that pub. Smith, who'd been away on his own account, turned up in the town one day clean broke, and in a deplorable state. He heard of Steelman's luck, and thought he was "all right", so went to his old friend.

Cold type—or any other kind of type—couldn't do justice to Steelman's disgust. To think that this was the reward of all the time and trouble he'd spent on Smith's education! However, when he cooled down, he said:

"Smith, you're a young man yet, and it's never too late to mend. There is still time for reformation. I can't help you now; it would only demoralize you altogether. To think, after the way I trained you, you can't battle round any better'n this! I always thought you were an irreclaimable mug, but I expected better things of you towards the end. I thought I'd make *something* of you. It's enough to dishearten any man and disgust him with the world. Why! you ought to be a rich man now with the chances and training you had! To think—but I won't talk of that; it has made me ill. I suppose I'll have to give you something, if it's only to get rid of the sight of you. Here's a quid, and I'm a mug for giving it to you. It'll do you more harm than good; and it ain't a friendly thing nor the right thing for me—who always had your welfare at heart—to give it to you under the circumstances. Now, get away out of my sight, and don't come near me till you've reformed. If you do, I'll have to stoush you out of regard for my own health and feelings."

But Steelman came down in the world again and picked up Smith on the road, and they battled round together for another year or so; and at last they were in Wellington—Steelman "flush" and stopping at an hotel, and Smith stumped, as usual, and staying with a friend. One night they were drinking together at the hotel, at the expense of some mugs whom Steelman was "educating". It was raining hard. When Smith was going home, he said:

"Look here, Steely, old man. Listen to the rain! I'll get wringing wet going home. You might as well lend me your overcoat tonight. You won't want it, and I won't hurt it."

And, Steelman's heart being warmed by his success, he lent the overcoat.

Smith went and pawned it, got glorious on the proceeds, and took the pawn-ticket to Steelman next day.

Smith had reformed.

His Mistake

THERE is one Chinaman the less in Australia by a mistake that was purely aboriginal. Perhaps he is missed in China. Ted Butler brings the account of the tragedy from Northern Queensland or somewhere.

The old shepherd had died, or got drunk, or got rats, or got the sack, or a legacy, or got sane, or chucked it, or got lost, or found, or a wife, or had cut his throat, or hanged himself, or got into Parliament or the peerage—anyway, anything had happened to him than can happen to an old shepherd or any other man in the bush, and he wasn't there.

Then a Chinaman came from nowhere, with nothing, apparently, save a suit of dungaree, basket boots and hat, and a smile that was three thousand years old. He looked as if he had fallen out of China last night, and had been blown all the way in a duststorm, and the cracked sweat and dust made him look more like an ancient joss. He had no English, but understood the boss as newchum Chinamen always understand bosses, or as bosses can always make them understand.

"You want a job?"

"Yel," said the Chinaman.

"Can you shepherd sheep?"

"Yel."

"You saw that hut along the track, where there were some sheep in the yard?"

"Yel."

"You go back there, and put the sheep out in the morning, and put them in at night."

"Yel."

"By and by I send you some ration."

"Yel."

"Well, stop yellin' and get."

"Yel."

"Get—go back."

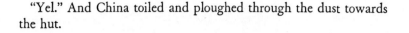

"Yel." And China toiled and ploughed through the dust towards the hut.

Presently Billy, the black boy, came riding home.

"I say, Billy."

"Yahs, boss."

"Don't take the saddle off yet. I want you to take some tucker along to the Mile Hut, and give it to the new shepherd you'll see there. Go to the storekeeper, and he'll give you a bag of ration."

"Yahs, boss."

But in about three-quarters of an hour Billy was back, and he brought the rations back with him.

"Wotinel, now, Billy? Didn't you see the new shepherd?"

"No, boss."

"Didn't you see anybody there at the hut?"

"No, boss."

"——it. Didn't you see a Chinaman there?"

"No, boss. What like it that phella?"

"X-X-X!——!!! Didn't you see a man—or a —— woman if you like? Didn't yer see any double dash thing?"

"No, boss." Then, as an afterthought. "I see it something. Yellow, like it dingo. Tail like it yarramin." (A horse. John had his pigtail down and loose, and was dressing it when Billy happened.) "Talk it like a plurry cockatoo. Bin killit sheep, mine think it. I bin kill it!"

I suppose they buried the Chow—and the boss carefully gave Billy an elementary lesson on the Races of Man before another blew out of China.

The Hypnotized Township

THEY said that Harry Chatswood, the mail contractor, would do anything for Cobb & Co., even to stretching fencing-wire across the road in a likely place: but I don't believe that—Harry was too good-hearted to risk injuring innocent passengers, and he had a fellow feeling for drivers, being an old coach-driver on rough outback tracks himself. But he did rig up fencing-wire for old Mac, the carrier, one night, though not across the road. Harry, by the way, was a city-born bushman, who had been everything for some years. Anything from six-foot-six to six-foot-nine, fourteen stone, and a hard case. He is a very successful coach-builder now, for he knows the wood, the roads, and the weak parts in a coach.

It was in the good seasons when competition was keen and men's hearts were hard—not as it is in times of drought, when there is no competition, and men's hearts are soft, and there is all kindness and goodwill between them. He had had much opposition in fighting Cobb & Co., and his coaches had won through on the outer tracks. There was little malice in his composition, but when old Mac, the teamster, turned his teams over to his sons and started a light van for parcels and passengers out from Cunnamulla (that place which always sounds to me suggestive of pumpkin pies), in seeming opposition to Harry Chatswood, Harry was annoyed.

Perhaps Mac only wished to end his days on the road with parcels that were light and easy to handle (not like loads of fencing-wire) and passengers that were sociable; but he had been doing well with his teams, and, besides, Harry thought he was after the mail contract: so Harry was annoyed more than he was injured. Mac was mean with the money he had—not because of the money he had a chance of getting; and he mostly slept in his van, in all weathers, when away from home, which was kept by his wife about half-way between the half-way house and the next "township".

One dark, gusty evening, Harry Chatswood's coach dragged, heavily though passengerless, into Cunnamulla, and, as he turned into the yard of the local Royal, he saw Mac's tilted four-wheeler (which he called his "van") drawn up opposite by the kerbing round the post office. Mac always chose a central position—with a vague idea of advertisement perhaps. But the nearness to the P.O. reminded Harry of the mail contracts, and he knew that Mac had taken up a passenger or two and some parcels in front of him (Harry) on the trip in. And something told Harry that Mac was asleep inside his van. It was a windy night, with signs of rain, and the curtains were drawn close.

Old Mac was there all right, and sleeping the sleep of a tired driver after a long drowsy day on a hard box-seat, with little or no back railing to it. But there was a lecture on, or an exhibition of hypnotism or mesmerism—"a blanky spirit rappin' fake", they called it, run by "some blanker" in "the hall"; and when old Mac had seen to his horses, he thought he might as well drop in for half an hour and see what was going on. Being a Mac, he was, of course, theological, scientific, and argumentative. He saw some things which woke him up, challenged the performer to hypnotize him, was "operated" on or "fooled with" a bit, had a "numb sorter light-headed feelin'", and was told by a voice from the back of the hall that his "leg was being pulled, Mac", and by another buzzin' far-away kind of "ventrillick" voice that he would make a good subject, and that, if he only had the will power and knew how (which he would learn from a book the professor had to sell for five shillings) he would be able to drive his van without horses or anything, save the pole sticking straight out in front. These weren't the professor's exact words—— But, anyway, Mac came to himself with a sudden jerk, left with a great Scottish snort of disgust and the sound of heavy boots along the floor; and after a resentful whisky at the Royal, where they laughed at his scrooging bushy eyebrows, fierce black eyes and his deadly-in-earnest denunciation of all humbugs and impostors, he returned to the aforesaid van, let down the flaps, buttoned the daft and "feekle" world out, and himself in, and then retired some more and slept, as I have said, rolled in his blankets and overcoats on a bed of cushions and chaff-bags.

Harry Chatswood got down from his empty coach, and was help-ing the yard-boy take out the horses, when his eye fell on the rem-nant of a roll of fencing-wire standing by the stable wall in the light of the lantern. Then an idea struck him unexpectedly, and his mind became luminous. He unhooked the swingle-bar, swung it up over his leader's rump (he was driving only three horses that trip), and hooked it on to the horns of the hames. Then he went inside (there was another light there) and brought out a bridle and an old pair of spurs that were hanging on the wall. He buckled on the spurs at the chopping-block, slipped the winkers off the leader and the bridle on, and took up the fencing-wire, and started out the gate with the horse. The boy gaped after him once, and then hurried to put up the other two horses. He knew Harry Chatswood, and was in a hurry to see what he would be up to.

There was a good crowd in town for the show, or the races, or a stock sale, or land ballot, or something; but most of them were tired, or at tea—or in the pubs—and the corners were deserted. Observe how fate makes time and things fit when she wants to do a good turn—or play a practical joke. Harry Chatswood, for instance, didn't know anything about the hypnotic business.

It was the corners of the main street or road and the principal short cross street, and the van was opposite the pub stables in the main street. Harry crossed the streets diagonally to the opposite corner, in a line with the van. There he slipped the bar down over the horse's rump, and fastened one end of the wire on to the ring of it. Then he walked back to the van, carrying the wire and letting the coils go wide, and, as noiselessly as possible, made a loop in the loose end and slipped it over the hooks on the end of the pole. ("Unnecessary detail!" my contemporaries will moan, "Overloaded with uninteresting details!" But that's because they haven't got the details—and it's the details that go.) Then Harry skipped back to his horse, jumped on, gathered up the bridle reins, and used his spurs. There was a swish and a clang, a scrunch and a clock-clock and rattle of wheels, and a surprised human sound; then a bump and a shout—for there was no underground drainage, and the gutters belong to the Stone Age. There was a swift clocking and rattle, more shouts, another bump, and a yell. And so on down the longish main street. The stable-boy, who had left the horses in his excitement, burst into the bar, shouting, "The Hypnertism's on, the Mesmerism's on! Ole Mac's van's runnin' away with him without no horses all right!" The crowd scuffled out into the street; there were some unfortunate horses hanging up of course at the panel by the pub trough, and the first to get to them jumped on and rode; the rest ran. The hall—where they were clearing the willing professor out in favour of a "darnce"—and the other pubs decanted their contents, and chance souls skipped for the verandas of weatherboard shanties out of which other souls popped to see the runaway. They saw a weird horseman, or rather, something like a camel (for Harry rode low, like Tod Sloan with his long back humped—for effect)—apparently fleeing for its life in a veil of dust, along the long white road, and some forty rods behind, an unaccountable tilted coach careered in its own separate cloud of dust. And from it came the shouts and yells. Men shouted and swore, women screamed for their children, and kids whimpered. Some of the men turned with an oath and stayed the panic with:

"It's only one of them flamin' motor-cars, you fools."

It might have been, and the yells the warning howls of a motorist who had burst or lost his honk-honk and his head.

"It's runnin' away!" or "The toff's mad or drunk!" shouted others. "It'll break its crimson back over the bridge."

"Let it!" was the verdict of some. "It's all the crimson carnal things are good for."

But the riders still rode and the footmen ran. There was a clatter of hoofs on the short white bridge looming ghostly ahead, and then, at a weird interval, the rattle and rumble of wheels, with no hoof-beats accompanying. The yells grew fainter. Harry's leader was a good horse, of the rather heavy coach-horse breed, with a little of the racing blood in her, but she was tired to start with, and only excitement and fright at the feel of the "pull" of the twisting wire kept her up to that speed; and now she was getting winded, so half a mile or so beyond the bridge Harry thought it had gone far enough, and he stopped and got down. The van ran on a bit, of course, and the loop of the wire slipped off the hooks of the pole. The wire recoiled itself roughly along the dust nearly to the heels of Harry's horse. Harry grabbed up as much of the wire as he could claw for, took the mare by the neck with the other hand and vanished through the dense fringe of scrub off the road, till the wire caught and pulled him up; he stood still for a moment, in the black shadow on the edge of a little clearing, to listen. Then he fumbled with the wire until he got it untwisted, cast it off, and moved off silently with the mare across the soft rotten ground, and left her in a handy bush stockyard, to be brought back to the stables at a late hour that night—or rather an early hour next morning—by a jack-eroo stable-boy who would have two half-crowns in his pocket and afterthought instructions to look out for that wire and hide it if possible.

Then Harry Chatswood got back quickly, by a roundabout way, and walked into the bar of the Royal, through the back entrance from the stables, and stared, and wanted to know where all the chaps had gone to, and what the noise was about, and whose trap had run away, and if anybody was hurt.

The growing crowd gathered round the van, silent and awestruck, and some of them threw off their hats, and lost them, in their anxiety to show respect for the dead, or render assistance to the hurt, as men do, round a bad accident in the bush. They got the old man out, and two of them helped him back along the road, with great solicitude, while some walked round the van, and swore beneath their breaths, or stared at it with open mouths, or examined it curiously, with their eyes only, and in breathless silence. They muttered, and agreed, in the pale moonlight now showing, that the sounds of the horses' hoofs had only been "spirit-rappin' sounds"; and, after some more muttering, two of the stoutest, with subdued oaths, laid hold of the pole and drew the van to the side of the road, where it would be out of the way of chance night traffic. But they stretched and rubbed their arms afterwards, and then, and on the way back, they swore to admiring acquaintances that they felt the "blanky 'lectricity" runnin' all up their arms and "elbers" while they were holding the pole, which, doubtless, they did—in imagination.

They got old Mac back to the Royal, with sundry hasty whiskies on the way. He was badly shaken, both physically, mentally, and in his convictions, and, when he'd pulled himself together, he had little to add to what they already knew. But he confessed that, when he got under his possum rug in the van, he couldn't help thinking of the professor and his creepy (it was "creepy", or "uncanny", or "awful", or "rum" with 'em now)—his blanky creepy hypnotism: and he (old Mac) had just laid on his back comfortable, and stretched his legs out straight, and his arms down straight by his sides, and drew long, slow breaths, and tried to fix his mind on nothing—as the professor had told him when he was "operatin' on him" in the hall. Then he began to feel a strange sort of numbness coming over him, and his limbs went heavy as lead, and he seemed to be gettin' lightheaded. Then, all on a sudden, his arms seemed to begin to lift, and just when he was goin' to pull 'em down the van started as they had heard and seen it. After a while he got on to his knees and managed to wrench a corner of the front curtain clear of the button and get his head out. And there was the van going helter-skelter, and feeling like Tam o'Shanter's mare (the old man said), and he on her bare-backed. And there was no horses, but a cloud of dust—or a spook—on ahead, and the bare pole steering straight for it, just as the professor had said it would be. The old man thought he was going to be taken clear across the Never-Never country and left to roast on a sandhill, hundreds of miles from anywhere, for his sins, and he said he was trying to think of a prayer or two all the time he was yelling. They handed him more whisky from the publican's own bottle. Hushed and cautious inquiries for the Professor (with a big P now) elicited the hushed and cautious fact that he had gone to bed. But old Mac caught the awesome name and glared round, so they hurriedly filled out another for him, from the boss's bottle. Then there was a slight commotion. The housemaid hurried scaredly into the bar behind and whispered to the boss. She had been startled nearly out of her wits by the Professor suddenly appearing at his bedroom door and calling upon her to have a stiff nobbler of whisky hot sent up to his room. The jackeroo yard-boy, aforesaid, volunteered to take it up, and while he was gone there were hints of hysterics from the kitchen, and the boss whispered in his turn to the crowd over the bar. The jackeroo just handed the tray and glass in through the partly opened door, had a glimpse of pyjamas, and after what seemed an interminable wait, he came tiptoeing into the bar amongst its awe-struck haunters with an air of great mystery, and no news whatever.

They fixed old Mac on a shake-down in the Commercial Room, where he'd have light and some overflow guests on the sofas for company. With a last whisky in the bar, and a stiff whisky by his side on the floor, he was understood to chuckle to the effect that he knew he was all right when he'd won "the keystone o' the brig". Though how a wooden bridge with a level plank floor could have a keystone I don't know—and they were too much impressed by the event of the evening to inquire. And so, with a few cases of hysterics to occupy the attention of the younger women, some whimpering of frightened children and comforting or chastened nagging by mothers, some unwonted prayers muttered secretly and forgettingly, and a good deal of subdued blasphemy, Cunnamulla sank to its troubled slumbers—some of the sleepers in the commercial and billiard-rooms and parlours at the Royal to start up in a cold sweat, out of their beery and hypnotic nightmares, to find Harry Chatswood making elaborate and fearsome passes over them with his long, gaunt arms and hands, and a flaming red table-cloth tied round his neck.

To be done with old Mac, for the present. He made one or two more trips, but always by daylight, taking care to pick up a swagman or a tramp when he had no passenger; but his conveections" had had too much of a shaking, so he sold his turn-out (privately and at a distance, for it was beginning to be called "the haunted van") and returned to his teams—always keeping one of the lads with him for company. He reckoned it would take the devil's own hypnotism to move a load of fencing-wire, or pull a wool-team of bullocks out of a bog; and before he invoked the ungodly power— which he let them believe he could—he'd stick there and starve till he and his bullocks died a "natural" death. (He was a bit Irish—as all Scots are—back on one side.)

But the strangest is to come. The Professor, next morning, proved uncomfortably unsociable, and though he could have done a roaring business that night—and for a week of nights after, for that matter —and though he was approached several times, he, for some mysterious reason known only to himself, flatly refused to give one more performance, and said he was leaving the town that day. He couldn't get a vehicle of any kind, for fear, love, or money, until Harry Chatswood, who took a day off, volunteered, for a stiff consideration, to borrow a buggy and drive him (the Professor) to the next town towards the then railway terminus, in which town the Professor's fame was not so awesome, and where he might get a lift to the railway. Harry ventured to remark to the Professor once or twice during the drive that "there was a rum business with old Mac's van last night", but he could get nothing out of him, so gave it best, and finished the journey in contemplative silence.

Now, the fact was that the Professor had been the most surprised and startled man in Cunnamulla that night; and he brooded over the thing till he came to the conclusion that hypnotism was a dangerous power to meddle with unless a man was physically and financially strong and carefree—which he wasn't. So he threw it up.

He learnt the truth, some years later, from a brother of Harry Chatswood, in a Home or Retreat for Geniuses, where "friends were paying", and his recovery was so sudden that it surprised and disappointed the doctor and his friend, the manager of the home. As it was, the Professor had some difficulty in getting out of it.

A Prisoner

THERE was an old prisoner—he might have been the last of the convicts—who used to drive the governmental cow to and fro, in the early morning, and in the gloaming, and milk, and garden, and clean up, and potter round about the post office or the jail (at opposite ends of the town) all day.

Our acquaintanceship began one fine morning, about half past eight, as I was waiting for the delivery window to open. He was sweeping round the basement, and remarked casually to his broom that my pipe made his mouth water. I got him a clay and a stick of twist. His conversation was slow, and on abstract subjects, and not nearly so interesting to me as his personality—but harmless and restful. He said he hadn't made up his mind what he'd do or where he'd go when he lost his billet. The broad arrows on his uniform were faded and faint, scarcely distinguishable at a short distance. He remarked that he'd have to get his "arrers" touched up a bit— they come out in the washin'. It was a strange acquaintanceship (and vague), now I come to think of it. I heard afterwards that there was a penalty of five pounds "hangin'" to it as far as I was concerned—I never heard what he'd have got—it might have cost him his place. But the constable never thought to mention the matter to me. There seemed something vaguely kind about Albany in this respect. Are the poor and unfortunate better off, out of jail, in new democratic places?

The jail cow was a pretty, plump, contented little white one, whose dignity didn't appear to suffer in the slightest degree by the fact of her being driven and milked by a felon. The felon's face was round and calm, with something bovine in expression—a suggestion as of a successful and contented farmer—but perhaps this came with the milking job. Whatever may have been his sins, sorrows, and sufferings, loves, hates, and wrongs in the past, his face and words gave no hint of them. I didn't see him this last time I was in Albany. Perhaps he'd got the sack. Anyway—I hope he gets enough tobacco.

I once—to break a howling silence (or for the want of some business of my own to occupy my mind)—asked the oldest inhabitant why the stowaway prisoners and others, who worked restfully on the roads without any visible guard over them, didn't clear out. He scratched behind his ear, thought, and said, "Wheres?" His intellect laboured a little longer, and the result was, "Wot do they want to clear out for?" That silenced me. Also, where would they be able to get plain clothes? The old resident (who told few lies, for he seldom talked, and probably wouldn't have known one when he told it) followed me up leisurely for a quarter of a mile or so, and wanted to know why I wanted to know why the convicts didn't clear out! This scared me, but now I think it was only his intellect starting to work for the first time in his life—the dawn of curiosity. Anyway, I pulled myself together, and told him that I asked the question because I was thinking about going to jail myself, and wanted to know. I reckon that stunned his intellect for another ten years.

Mitchell: A Character Sketch

IT was a very mean station, and Mitchell thought he had better go himself and beard the overseer for tucker. His mates were waiting till the overseer went out on the run, and then trying their luck with the cook; but the self-assertive and diplomatic Mitchell decided to go.

"Good day," said Mitchell.

"Good day," said the manager.

"It's hot," said Mitchell.

"Yes, it's hot."

"I don't suppose," said Mitchell; "I don't suppose it's any use asking you for a job?"

"Naw."

"Well, I won't ask you," said Mitchell, "but I don't suppose you want any fencing done?"

"Naw."

"Nor boundary-riding?"

"Naw."

"You ain't likely to want a man to knock round?"

"Naw."

"I thought not. Things are pretty bad just now."

"Na—yes—they are."

"Ah, well; there's a lot to be said on the squatter's side as well as the men's. I suppose I can get a bit of rations?"

"Ye-yes," (Shortly)—"Wot d'yer want?"

"Well, let's see; we want a bit of meat and flour—I think that's all. Got enough tea and sugar to carry us on."

"All right. Cook! have you got any meat?"

"No!"

To Mitchell: "Can you kill a sheep?"

"Rather!"

To the cook: "Give this man a cloth and knife and steel, and let him go up to the yard and kill a sheep." (To Mitchell): "You can take a forequarter and get a bit of flour."

Half an hour later Mitchell came back with the carcass wrapped in the cloth.

"Here yer are; here's your sheep," he said to the cook.

"That's all right; hang it in there. Did you take a forequarter?"

"No."

"Well, why didn't you? The boss told you to."

"I didn't want a forequarter. I don't like it. I took a hindquarter." So he had.

The cook scratched his head; he seemed to have nothing to say. He thought about trying to think, perhaps, but gave it best. It was too hot and he was out of practice.

"Here, fill these up, will you?" said Mitchell. "That's the tea-bag, and that's the sugar-bag, and that's the flour-bag."

He had taken them from the front of his shirt.

"Don't be frightened to stretch 'em a little, old man. I've got two mates to feed."

The cook took the bags mechanically and filled them well before he knew what he was doing. Mitchell talked all the time.

"Thank you," said he—"got a bit of baking-powder?"

"Ye—yes, here you are."

"Thank you. Find it dull here, don't you?"

"Well, yes, pretty dull. There's a bit of cooked beef and some bread and cake there, if you want it!"

"Thanks," said Mitchell, sweeping the broken victuals into an old pillow-slip which he carried on his person for such an emergency. "I s'pose you find it dull round here."

"Yes, pretty dull."

"No one to talk to much?"

"No, not many."

"Tongue gets rusty?"

"Ye—es, sometimes."

"Well, so long, and thank yer."

"So long," said the cook (he nearly added "thank yer").

"Well, good day; I'll see you again."

"Good day."

Mitchell shouldered his spoil and left.

The cook scratched his head; he had a chat with the overseer afterwards, and they agreed that the traveller was a bit gone.

But Mitchell's head wasn't gone—not much: he had been round a bit—that was all.

Ease Without Opulence

The Shanty-keeper's Wife

THERE were about a dozen ot us jammed into the coach, on the box-seat and hanging on to the roof and tailboard as best we could. We were shearers, bagmen, agents, a squatter, a cockatoo, the usual joker—and one or two professional spielers, perhaps. We were tired and stiff and nearly frozen—too cold to talk and too irritable to risk the inevitable argument which an interchange of ideas would have led up to. We had been looking forword for hours, it seemed, to the pub where we were. to change horses. For the last hour or two all that our united efforts had been able to get out of the driver was a grunt to the effect that it was " 'bout a couple o' miles". Then he said, or grunted, " 'Tain't fur now," a couple of times, and refused to commit himself any further; he seemed grumpy about having committed himself so far.

He was one of those men who take everything in dead earnest; who regard any expression of ideas outside their own sphere of life as trivial, or, indeed, if addressed directly to them, as offensive; who, in fact, are darkly suspicious of anything in the shape of a joke or laugh on the part of an outsider in their own particular dust-hole. He seemed to be always thinking, and thinking a lot; when his hands were not both engaged, he would tilt his hat forward and scratch the base of his skull with his little finger, and let his jaw hang. But his intellectual powers were mostly concentrated on a doubtful swingle-tree, a misfitting collar, or that there bay or piebald (on the off or near side) with the sore shoulder.

Casual letters or papers, to be delivered on the road, were matters which troubled him vaguely, but constantly—like the abstract ideas of his passengers.

The joker of our party was a humorist of the dry order, and had been slyly taking rises out of the driver for the last two or three stages. But the driver only brooded. He wasn't the one to tell you straight if you offended him, or if you fancied you offended him, and thus gain your respect, or prevent a misunderstanding which would result in lifelong enmity. He might meet you in after years when you had forgotten all about your trespass—if indeed you had ever

155

been conscious of it—and stoush you unexpectedly on the ear.

Also you might regard him as your friend, on occasion, and yet he would stand by and hear a perfect stranger tell you the most outrageous lies, to your hurt, and know that the stranger was telling lies, and never put you up to it. It would never enter his head to do so. It wouldn't be any affair of his—only an abstract question.

It grew darker and colder. The rain came as if the frozen south were spitting at our face and neck and hands, and our feet grew as big as camels', and went dead, and we might as well have stamped the footboards with wooden legs for all the feeling we got into our own. But they were more comfortable that way, for the toes didn't curl up and pain so much, nor did our corns stick out so hard against the leather, and shoot.

We looked out eagerly for some clearing, or fence, or light—some sign of the shanty where we were to change horses—but there was nothing save blackness all round. The long, straight, cleared road was no longer relieved by the ghostly patch of light, far ahead, where the bordering tree-walls came together in perspective and framed the ether. We were down in the bed of the bush.

We pictured a haven of rest with a suspended lamp burning in the frosty air outside and a big log fire in a cosy parlour off the bar, and a long table set for supper. But this is a land of contradictions; wayside shanties turn up unexpectedly, and in the most unreasonable places, and are, as likely as not, prepared for a banquet when you are not hungry and can't wait, and as cold and dark as a bushman's grave when you are and can.

Suddenly the driver said: "We're there now." He said this as if he had driven us to the scaffold to be hanged, and was fiercely glad that he'd got us there safely at last. We looked, but saw nothing; then a light appeared ahead and seemed to come towards us; and presently we saw that it was a lantern held up by a man in a slouch hat, with a dark bushy beard, and a three-bushel bag around his shoulders. He held up his other hand, and said something to the driver in a tone that might have been used by the leader of a search party who had just found the body. The driver stopped and then went on slowly.

"What's up?" we asked. "What's the trouble?"

"Oh, it's all right," said the driver.

"The publican's wife is sick," somebody said, "and he wants us to come quietly."

The usual little slab-and-bark shanty was suggested in the gloom, with a big bark stable looming in the background. We climbed down like so many cripples. As soon as we began to feel our legs and be sure we had the right ones and the proper allowance of feet, we helped, as quietly as possible, to take the horses out and round to the stable.

"Is she very bad?" we asked the publican, showing as much concern as we could.

"Yes," he said, in the subdued voice of a rough man who had spent several anxious, sleepless nights by the sick-bed of a dear one. "But, God willing, I think we'll pull her through."

Thus encouraged, we said sympathetically: "We're very sorry to trouble you, but I suppose we could manage to get a drink and a bit to eat?"

"Well," he said, "there's nothing to eat in the house, and I've only got rum and milk. You can have that if you like."

One of the pilgrims broke out here.

"Well, of all the pubs," he began, "that I've ever——"

"Hush-sh-sh!" said the publican.

The pilgrim scowled and retired to the rear. You can't express your feelings freely when there's a woman dying close handy.

"Well, who says rum and milk?" asked the joker in a low voice.

"Wait here," said the publican, and disappeared into the little front passage.

Presently a light showed through a window with a scratched and fly-bitten B and A on two panes, and a mutilated R on the third, which was broken. A door opened, and we sneaked into the bar. It was like having drinks after hours where the police are strict and independent.

When we came out the driver was scratching his head and looking at the harness on the veranda floor.

"You fellows'll have ter put in the time for an hour or so. The horses is outback somewheres," and he indicated the interior of Australia with a side jerk of his head, "and the boy ain't back with 'em yet."

"But dash it all," said the pilgrim, "me and my mate——"

"Hush!" said the publican.

"How long are the horses likely to be?" we asked the driver.

"Dunno," he grunted. "Might be three or four hours. It's all accordin'."

157

"Now, look here," said the pilgrim, "me and my mate wanter catch the train."

"Hush-sh-sh!" from the publican in a fierce whisper.

"Well, boss," said the joker, "can you let us have beds, then? I don't want to freeze here all night, anyway."

"Yes," said the landlord, "I can do that, but some of you will have to sleep double and some of you'll have to take it out of the sofas, and one or two'll have to make a shake-down on the floor. There's plenty of bags in the stable, and you've got rugs and coats with you. Fix it up amongst yourselves."

"But look here!" interrupted the pilgrim, desperately, "we can't afford to wait! We're only battlers, me and my mate, pickin' up crumbs by the wayside. We've got to catch the——"

"Hush!" said the publican, savagely. "You fool, didn't I tell you my missus was bad? I won't have any noise."

"But look here," protested the pilgrim, "we must catch the train at Dead Camel——"

"You'll catch my boot presently," said the publican, with a savage oath, "and go further than Dead Camel. I won't have my missus disturbed for you or any other man! Just you shut up or get out, and take your blooming mate with you."

We lost patience with the pilgrim and sternly took him aside.

"Now, for God's sake, hold your jaw," we said. "Haven't you got any consideration at all? Can't you see the man's wife is ill—dying perhaps—and he nearly worried off his head?"

The pilgrim and his mate were scraggy little bipeds of the city push variety, so they were suppressed.

"Well," yawned the joker, "I'm not going to roost on a stump all night. I'm going to turn in."

"It'll be eighteenpence each," hinted the landlord. "You can settle now, if you like, to save time."

We took the hint, and had another drink. I don't know how we "fixed it up amongst ourselves", but we got settled down somehow. There was a lot of mysterious whispering and scuffling round by the light of a couple of dirty greasy bits of candle. Fortunately we dared not speak loud enough to have a row, though most of us were by this time in the humour to pick a quarrel with a long-lost brother.

The joker got the best bed, as good-humoured, good-natured chaps generally do, without seeming to try for it. The growler of the party got the floor and chaff-bags, as selfish men mostly do—

without seeming to try for it either. I took it out of one of the sofas, or rather that sofa took it out of me. It was short and narrow and down by the head, with a leaning to one corner on the outside, and had more nails and bits of gin-case than original sofa in it.

I had been asleep for three seconds, it seemed, when somebody shook me by the shoulder and said:

"Take yer seats."

When I got out, the driver was on the box, and the others were getting rum and milk inside themselves (and in bottles) before taking their seats.

It was colder and darker than ever and the South Pole seemed nearer; and pretty soon, but for the rum, we should have been in a worse fix than before.

There was a spell of grumbling. Presently someone said:

"I don't believe them horses was lost at all. I was round behind the stable before I went to bed, and seen horses there; and if they wasn't them same horses there, I'll eat 'em raw!"

"Would yer?" said the driver, in a disinterested tone.

"I would," said the passenger. Then, with a sudden ferocity, "And you too!"

The driver said nothing. It was an abstract question which didn't interest him.

We saw that we were on delicate ground, and changed the subject for a while. Then someone else said:

"I wonder where his missus was? I didn't see any signs of her about, or any other woman about the place, and we was pretty well all over it."

"Must have kept her in the stable," suggested the joker.

"No, she wasn't, for Scotty and that chap on the roof was there after bags."

"She might have been in the loft," reflected the joker.

"There was no loft," put in a voice from the top of the coach.

"I say, Mister—Mister man," said the joker suddenly to the driver, "was his missus sick at all?"

"I dunno," replied the driver. "She might have been. He said so, anyway. I ain't got no call to call a man a liar."

"See here," said the cannibalistic individual to the driver, in the tone of a man who has made up his mind for a row, "has that shanty-keeper got a wife at all?"

"I believe he has."

159

"And is she living with him?"

"No, she ain't—if yer wanter know."

"Then where is she?"

"I dunno. How am I to know? She left him three or four years ago. She was in Sydney last time I heard of her. It ain't no affair of mine, anyways."

"And is there any woman about the place at all, driver?" inquired a professional wanderer reflectively.

"No—not that I knows of. There useter be an old black gin come pottering round sometimes, but I ain't seen her lately."

"And excuse me, driver, but is there anyone round there at all?" inquired the professional wanderer, with the air of a conscientious writer, collecting material for an Australian novel from life, and with an eye to detail.

"Naw," said the driver—and recollecting that he was expected to be civil and obliging to his employers' patrons, he added in surly apology, "Only the boss and the stableman, that I knows of." Then, repenting of the apology, he asserted his manhood again, and asked, in a tone calculated to risk a breach of the peace, "Any more questions, gentlemen—while the shop's open?"

There was a long pause.

"Driver," asked the pilgrim appealingly, "was them horses lost at all?"

"I dunno," said the driver. "He said they was. He's got the looking after them. It was nothing to do with me."

"Twelve drinks at sixpence a drink"—said the joker, as if calculating to himself—"that's six bob, and, say on an average, four shouts —that's one pound four. Twelve beds at eighteenpence a bed—that's eighteen shillings; and say ten bob in various drinks and the stuff we brought with us, that's two pound twelve. That publican didn't do so bad out of us in two hours."

We wondered how much the driver got out of it, but thought it best not to ask him.

We didn't say much for the rest of the journey. There was the usual man who thought as much and knew all about if from the first, but he wasn't appreciated. We suppressed him. One or two wanted to go back and stoush that landlord, and the driver stopped the coach cheerfully at their request; but they said they'd come across him again, and allowed themselves to be persuaded out of it. It made us feel bad to think how we had allowed ourselves to be delayed, and robbed, and had sneaked round on tiptoe, and how we had sat on the inoffensive pilgrim and his mate, and all on account of a sick wife who didn't exist.

The coach arrived at Dead Camel in an atmosphere of mutual suspicion and distrust, and we spread ourselves over the train and departed.

Two Dogs and a Fence

"NOTHING makes a dog madder," said Mitchell, "than to have another dog come outside his fence and sniff and bark at him through cracks when he can't get out. The other dog might be an entire stranger; he might be an old chum, and he mightn't bark—only sniff—but it makes no difference to the inside dog. The inside dog generally starts it, and the outside dog only loses his temper and gets wild because the inside dog has lost *his* and got mad and made such a stinking fuss about nothing at all; and then the outside dog barks back and makes matters a thousand times worse, and the inside dog foams at the mouth and dashes the foam about, and goes at it like a million steel traps.

"I can't tell why the inside dog gets so wild about it in the first place, except, perhaps, because he thinks the outside dog has taken him at a disadvantage and is 'poking it at him'; anyway, he gets madder the longer it lasts, and at last he gets savage enough to snap off his own tail and tear it to bits, because he can't get out and chew up that other dog; and if he did get out he'd kill the other dog, or try to, even if it was his own brother.

"Sometimes the outside dog only smiles and trots off; sometimes he barks back good-naturedly; sometimes he only gives a couple of disinterested barks as if he isn't particular, but is expected, because of his dignity and doghood, to say something under the circumstances; and sometimes, if the outside dog is a little dog, he'll get away from that fence in a hurry on the first surprise, or, if he's a cheeky little dog, he'll first make sure that the inside dog can't get out, and then he'll have some fun.

"It's amusing to see a big dog, of the Newfoundland kind, sniffing along outside a fence with a broad, good-natured grin on his face all the time the inside dog is whooping away at the rate of thirty whoops a second, and choking himself, and covering himself with foam, and dashing the spray through the cracks, and jolting and jerking every joint in his body up to the last joint in his tail.

"Sometimes the inside dog is a little dog, and the smaller he is the more row he makes—but then he knows he's safe. And sometimes,

as I said before, the outside dog is a short-tempered dog who hates
a row, and never wants to have a disagreement with anybody—
like a good many peaceful men, who hate rows, and are always
nice and civil and pleasant, in a nasty, unpleasant, surly, sneering
sort of civil way that makes you want to knock their heads off;
men who never start a row, but keep it going, and make it a thous-
and times worse when it's once started, just because they didn't
start it—and keep on saying so, and that the other party did. The
short-tempered outside dog gets wild at the other dog for losing his
temper, and says:

"'What are you making such a fuss about? What's the matter
with you, anyway? Hey?'

"And the inside dog says:

"'Who do you think you're talking to? You——! I'll——' etc.,
etc., etc.

"Then the outside dog says:

"'Why, you're worse than a flaming old slut!'

"*Then* they go at it, and you can hear them miles off, like a
Chinese war—like a hundred great guns firing eighty blank cart-
ridges a minute, till the outside dog is just as wild to get inside and
eat the inside dog as the inside dog is to get out and disembowel
him. Yet if those same two dogs were to meet casually outside they
might get chummy at once, and be the best of friends, and swear
everlasting mateship, and take each other home."

The Songs They Used to Sing

ON the diggings up to twenty-odd years ago—and as far back as I can remember—on Lambing Flat, Pipeclay, Gulgong, Home Rule, and so through the roaring list; in bark huts, tents, public-houses, sly-grog shanties, and—well, the most glorious voice of all belonged to a bad girl. We were only children and didn't know why she was bad, but we weren't allowed to play near or go near the hut she lived in, and we were trained to believe firmly that something awful would happen to us if we stayed to answer a word, and didn't run away as fast as our legs could carry us, if she attempted to speak to us. We had before us the dread example of one urchin, who got an awful hiding and went on bread and water for twenty-four hours for allowing her to kiss him and give him lollies. She didn't look bad—she looked to us like a grand and beautiful lady-girl—but we got instilled into us the idea that she was an awful bad woman, something more terrible even than a drunken man, and one whose presence was to be feared and fled from. There were two other girls in the hut with her, also a pretty little girl, who called her Auntie, and with whom we were not allowed to play—for they were all bad; which puzzled us as much as child-minds can be puzzled. We couldn't make out how everybody in one house could be bad. We used to wonder why these bad people weren't hunted away or put in jail if they were so bad. And another thing puzzled us. Slipping out after dark, when the bad girls happened to be singing in their house, we'd sometimes run against men hanging round the hut by ones and twos and threes, listening. They seemed mysterious. They were mostly good men, and we concluded they were listening and watching the bad women's house to see that they didn't kill anyone, or steal and run away with any bad little boys—ourselves, for instance—who ran out after dark; which, as we were informed, those bad people were always on the lookout for a chance to do.

We were told in after years that old Peter McKenzie (a respectable, married, hard-working digger) would sometimes steal up opposite the bad door in the dark, and throw in money done up

in a piece of paper, and listen round until the bad girl had sung
"The Bonnie Hills of Scotland" two or three times. Then he'd go
and get drunk, and stay drunk two or three days at a time. And
his wife caught him throwing the money in one night, and there
was a terrible row, and she left him; and people always said it was
all a mistake. But we couldn't see the mistake then.

But I can hear that girl's voice through the night, twenty years
ago:

> *Oh! the bloomin' heath, and the pale blue bell,*
>   *In my bonnet then I wore;*
> *And memory knows no brighter theme*
>   *Than those happy days of yore.*
> *Scotland! Land of chief and song!*
> *Oh, what charms to thee belong!*

And I am old enough to understand why poor Peter McKenzie
—who was married to a Saxon, and a Tartar—went and got drunk
when the bad girl sang "The Bonnie Hills of Scotland".

> *His anxious eye might look in vain*
> *For some loved form it knew!*

And yet another thing puzzled us greatly at the time. Next door
to the bad girl's house there lived a very respectable family—a
family of good girls with whom we were allowed to play, and from
whom we got lollies (those hard old red-and-white "fish lollies"
that grocers sent home with parcels of groceries and receipted bills).
Now one washing day, they being as glad to get rid of us at home
as we were to get out, we went over to the good house and found
no one at home except the grown-up daughter, who used to sing
for us, and read *Robinson Crusoe* of nights, "out loud", and give
us more lollies than any of the rest—and with whom we were
passionately in love, notwithstanding the fact that she was engaged
to a "grown-up man"—(we reckoned he'd be dead and out of the
way by the time we were old enough to marry her). She was washing. She had carried the stool and tub over against the stick fence
which separated her house from the bad house; and, to our astonishment and dismay, the bad girl had brought *her* tub over against
her side of the fence. They stood and worked with their shoulders
to the fence between them, and heads bent down close to it. The
bad girl would sing a few words, and the good girl after her, over

165

and over again. They sang very low, we thought. Presently the good grown-up girl turned her head and caught sight of us. She jumped, and her face went flaming red; she laid hold of the stool and carried it, tub and all, away from that fence in a hurry. And the bad grown-up girl took her tub back to her house. The good grown-up girl made us promise never to tell what we saw—that she'd been talking to a bad girl—else she would never, never marry us.

She told me, in after years, when she'd grown up to be a grand-mother, that the bad girl was surreptitiously teaching her to sing "Madeline" that day.

I remember a dreadful story of a digger who went and shot him-self one night after hearing that bad girl sing. We thought then what a frightfully bad woman she must be. The incident terrified us; and thereafter we kept carefully and fearfully out of reach of her voice, lest we should go and do what the digger did.

I have a dreamy recollection of a circus on Gulgong in the roaring days, more than twenty years ago, and a woman (to my child-fancy a being from another world) standing in the middle of the ring, singing:

> *Out in the cold world—out in the street—*
> *Asking a penny from each one I meet;*
> *Cheerless I wander about all the day,*
> *Wearing my young life in sorrow away!*

That last line haunted me for many years. I remember being frightened by women sobbing (and one or two great grown-up diggers also) that night in that circus.

"Father, Dear Father, Come Home with Me Now" was a sacred song then, not a peg for vulgar parodies and more vulgar "business" for fourth-rate clowns and corner-men. Then there was "The Prairie Flower". "Out on the prairie, in an early day"—I can hear the digger's wife yet: she was the prettiest girl on the field. They married on the sly and crept into camp after dark; but the diggers got wind of it and rolled up with gold-dishes and shovels, and gave them a real good tin-kettling in the old-fashioned style, and a nugget or two to start housekeeping on. She had a very sweet voice.

> *Fair as a lily, joyous and free,*
> *Light of the prairie home was she.*

She's a "granny" now, no doubt—or dead.

And I remember a poor, brutally ill-used little wife, wearing a black eye mostly, and singing "Love Amongst the Roses" at her work. And they sang the "Blue Tail Fly" and all the first and best coon songs—in the days when old John Brown sank a duffer on the hill.

The great bark kitchen of Granny Mathews's Redclay Inn. A fresh back-log thrown behind the fire, which lights the room fitfully. Company settled down to pipes, subdued yarning, and reverie.

Flash Jack—red sash, cabbage-tree hat on back of head with nothing in it, glossy black curls bunched up in front of brim. Flash Jack volunteers, without invitation, preparation, or warning, and through his nose:

> *Hoh!*
> *There was a wild kerlonial youth,*
>   *John Dowlin was his name!*
> *He bountied on his parients,*
>   *Who lived in Castlemaine!*

and so on to—

> *He took a pistol from his breast*
>   *And waved that lit—tle toy—*

"little toy" with an enthusiastic flourish and great unction on Flash Jack's part.

> *"I'll fight, but I won't surrender!" said*
>   *The wild Kerlonial Boy.*

Even this fails to rouse the company's enthusiasm. "Give us a song, Abe! Give us 'The Lowlands'!" Abe Mathews, bearded and grizzled, is lying on the broad of his back on a bench, with his hands clasped under his head—his favourite position for smoking, reverie, yarning, or singing. He had a strong, deep voice, which used to thrill me through and through, from hair to toenails, as a child.

They bother Abe till he takes his pipe out of his mouth and puts it behind his head on the end of the stool:

> *The ship was built in Glasgow;*
> *'Twas the "Golden Vanitee"—*

Lines have dropped out of my memory during the thirty years gone between:

And she ploughed in the Low Lands, Low!

The public-house people and more diggers drop into the kitchen, as all do within hearing, when Abe sings.

"Now then, boys":

And she ploughed in the Low Lands, Low!

"Now, all together!

The Low Lands! The Low Lands!
And she ploughed in the Low Lands, Low!

Toe and heel and flat of foot begin to stamp the clay floor, and horny hands to slap patched knees in accompaniment.

"Oh! save me, lads!" he cried,
"I'm drifting with the current,
And I'm drifting with the tide!
And I'm sinking in the Low Lands, Low!
The Low Lands! The Low Lands!"

The old bark kitchen is a-going now. Heels drumming on gin-cases under stools; hands, knuckles, pipe-bowls, and pannikins keeping time on the table.

And we sewed him in his hammock,
And we slipped him o'er the side,
And we sunk him in the Low Lands, Low!
The Low Lands! The Low Lands!
And we sunk him in the Low Lands, Low!

Old Boozer Smith—a dirty gin-sodden bundle of rags on the floor in the corner with its head on a candle-box, and covered by a horse-rug—old Boozer Smith is supposed to have been dead to the universe for hours past, but the chorus must have disturbed his torpor; for, with a suddenness and unexpectedness that makes the next man jump, there comes a bellow from under the horse-rug:

Wot though!—I wear!—a rag!—ged coat!
I'll wear it like a man!

and ceases as suddenly as it commenced. He struggles to bring his ruined head and bloated face above the surface, glares round; then, no one questioning his manhood, he sinks back and dies to creation;

and subsequent proceedings are only interrupted by a snore, as far
as he is concerned.

Little Jimmy Nowlett, the bullock-driver, is inspired. "Go on,
Jimmy! Give us a song!"

> *In the days when we were hard up*
> *For want of wood and wire—*

Jimmy always blunders; it should have been "food and fire"—

> *We used to tie our boots up*
> *With lit—tle bits—er wire;*

and—

> *I'm sitting in my lit—tle room,*
> *It measures six by six;*
> *The work-house wall is opposite,*
> *I've counted all the bricks!*

"Give us a chorus, Jimmy!"

Jimmy does, giving his head a short, jerky nod for nearly every
word, and describing a circle round his crown—as if he were
stirring a pint of hot tea—with his forefinger, at the end of every
line:

> *Hall!—Round!—Me—Hat!*
> *I wore a weepin' willer!*

Jimmy is a Cockney.
"Now then, boys!"

> *Hall—round—me—hat!*

How many old diggers remember it?
And:

> *A butcher, and a baker, and a quiet-looking Quaker,*
> *All a-courting pretty Jessie at the Railway Bar.*

I used to wonder as a child what the "railway bar" meant.
And:

> *I would, I would, I would in vain*
> *That I were single once again!*
> *But ah, alas, that will not be*
> *Till apples grow on the willow tree.*

A drunken gambler's young wife used to sing that song—to herself.

A stir at the kitchen door, and a cry of "Pinter!" and old Poynton, Ballarat digger, appears and is shoved in; he has several drinks aboard, and they proceed to "git Pinter on the singin' lay", and at last talk him round. He has a good voice, but no "theory", and blunders worse than Jimmy Nowlett with the words. He starts with a howl:

> *Hoh!*
> *Way down in Covent Gar-ar-r-dings*
>   *A-strolling I did go,*
> *To see the sweetest flow-ow-wers*
>   *That e'er in gardings grow.*

He saw the rose and lily—the red and white and blue—and he saw the sweetest flow-ow-ers that e'er in gardings grew; for he saw two lovely maidens (Pinter calls 'em "virgings") underneath (he must have meant on top of) "a garding chair", sings Pinter.

> *And one was lovely Jessie,*
> *With the jet black eyes and hair,*

roars Pinter,

> *And the other was a vir-ir-ging,*
> *I solemn'lye declare!*

"Maiden, Pinter!" interjects Mr Nowlett.

"Well, it's all the same," retorts Pinter. "A maiden *is* a virging, Jimmy. If you're singing, Jimmy, and not me, I'll leave off!" Chorus of "Order! Shut up, Jimmy!"

> *I quicklye step-ped up to her,*
>   *And unto her did sa-a-y:*
> *Do you belong to any young man*
>   *Hoh, tell me that, I pra-a-y?*

Her answer, according to Pinter, was surprisingly prompt and unconventional; also full and concise:

> *No; I belong to no young man—*
>   *I solemnlye declare!*
> *I mean to live a virging*
>   *And still my laurels wear!*

Jimmy Nowlett attempts to move an amendment in favour of "maiden", but is promptly suppressed. It seems that Pinter's suit has a happy termination, for he is supposed to sing in the character

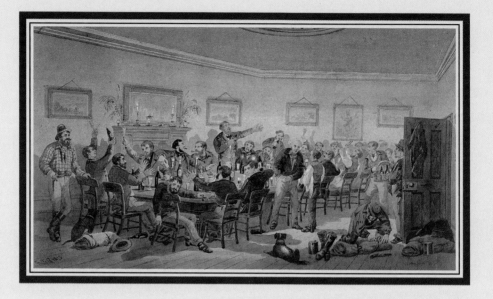

A Hilarious Dinner Party
Dixson Library, State Library of New South Wales

of a "Sailor Bold", and as he turns to pursue his stroll in "Covent
Gar-ar-dings":

"Oh, no! Oh, no! Oh, no!" she cried.
"I love a Sailor Bold!"

"Hong-kore, Pinter! Give us the 'Golden Glove', Pinter!"

Thus warmed up, Pinter starts with an explanatory "spoken" to
the effect that the song he is about to sing illustrates some of the
little ways of women, and how, no matter what you say or do, she
is bound to have her own way in the end; also how, in one instance,
she set about getting it.

Hoh!
Now, it's of a young squoire near Timworth did dwell,
Who courted a nobleman's daughter so well—

The song has little or nothing to do with the "squire", except so
far as "all friends and relations had given consent", and—

The troo-soo was ordered—appointed the day,
And a farmier were appointed for to give her away—

which last seemed a most unusual proceeding, considering the wedding was a toney affair; but perhaps there were personal interests—
the nobleman might have been hard up, and the farmer backing
him. But there was an extraordinary scene in the church, and things
got mixed.

For as soon as this maiding this farmier espied:
"Hoh, my heart! Hoh, my heart!
Hoh, my heart!" then she cried.

Hysterics? Anyway, instead of being wed—

This maiden took sick and she went to her bed.

(N.B.—Pinter sticks to "virging".)

Whereupon friends and relations and guests left the house in a
body (a strange but perhaps a wise proceeding, after all—maybe
they smelt a rat) and left her to recover alone, which she did
promptly. And then:

Shirt, breeches, and waistcoat this maiding put on,
And a-hunting she went with her dog and her gun,
She hunted all round where this farmier did dwell,
Because in her own heart she love-ed him well.

The cat's out of the bag now:

And often she fired, but no game she killed—

which is not surprising—

Till at last the young farmier came into the field—

No wonder. She put it to him straight:

"Oh, why are you not at the wedding?" she cried,
"For to wait on the squoire, and to give him his bride."

He was as prompt and as delightfully unconventional in his reply as the young lady in Covent Gardings:

"Oh, no! and oh, no! For the truth I must sa-a-y,
I love her too well for to give her a-w-a-a-y!"

which was satisfactory to the disguised "virging".

"... and I'd take sword in hand,
And by honour I'd win her if she would command."

Which was still more satisfactory.

Now this virging, being—

(Jimmy Nowlett: "Maiden, Pinter!"——Jim is thrown on a stool and sat on by several diggers.)

Now this maiding, being please-ed to see him so bold,
She gave him a glove that was flowered with gold,

and explained that she found it in his field while hunting around with her dog and her gun. It is understood that he promised to look up the owner. Then she went home and put an advertisement in the local *Herald,* and that ad. must have caused considerable sensation. She stated that she had lost her golden glove, and

The young man that finds it and brings it to me,
Hoh, that very young man my husband shall be!

She had a saving clause in case the young farmer mislaid the glove before he saw the ad., and an *old* bloke got holt of it and fetched it along. But everything went all right. The young farmer turned up with the glove. He was a very respectable young farmer, and expressed his gratitude to her for having "honour-ed him with her love". They were married, and the song ends with a picture of the young farmeress milking the cow, and the young farmer going whistling to plough. The fact that they lived and grafted on the selection proves that I hit the right nail on the head when I guessed, in the first place, that the old nobleman was "stony".

In after years,

> ... she told him of the fun,
> How she hunted him up with her dog and her gun.

But whether he was pleased or otherwise to hear it, after years of matrimonial experiences, the old song doesn't say, for it ends there.

Flash Jack is more successful with "Saint Patrick's Day".

> I come to the river, I jumped it quite clever,
> Me wife tumbled in, and I lost her for ever,
> St Patrick's own day in the mornin'!

This is greatly appreciated by Jimmy Nowlett, who is suspected, especially by his wife, of being more cheerful when on the roads than when at home.

"Sam Holt" was a great favourite with Jimmy Nowlett in after years.

> Oh, do you remember Black Alice, Sam Holt?
> Black Alice so dirty and dark—
> Who'd a nose on her face—I forget how it goes—
> And teeth like a Moreton Bay shark.

Sam Holt must have been very hard up for tucker as well as beauty then, for

> Do you remember the possums and grubs
> She baked for you down by the creek?

Sam Holt was, apparently, a hardened Flash Jack.

> You were not quite the cleanly potato, Sam Holt.

Reference is made to his "manner of holding a flush", and he is asked to remember several things which he, no doubt, would rather forget, including

> ... the hiding you got from the boys.

The song is decidedly personal.

But Sam Holt makes a pile and goes home, leaving many a better and worse man to pad the hoof outback. And—Jim Nowlett sang this with so much feeling as to make it appear a personal affair between him and the absent Holt—

> *And, don't you remember the fiver, Sam Holt,*
> *You borrowed so careless and free?*
> *I reckon I'll whistle a good many tunes*

(with increasing feeling)

> *Ere you think of that fiver and me.*

For the chances will be that Sam Holt's old mate

> *Will be humping his drum on the Hughenden Road*
> *To the end of the chapter of fate.*

An echo from "The Old Bark Hut", sung in the opposition camp across the gully:

> *You may leave the door ajar, but if you keep it shut,*
> *There's no need of suffocation in the Ould Barrk' Hut.*
> *The tucker's in the gin-case, but you'd better keep it shut—*
> *For the flies will canther round it in the Ould Barrk Hut.*

However:

> *What's out of sight is out of mind, in the Ould Barrk Hut.*
> *We washed our greasy moleskins*
> *On the banks of the Condamine.—*

Somebody tackled the "Old Bullock Dray"; it must be over fifty verses now. I saw a bushman at a country dance start to sing that song; he'd get up to ten or fifteen verses, break down, and start afresh. At last he sat down on his heel to it, in the centre of the clear floor, resting his wrist on his knee, and keeping time with an index finger. It was very funny, but the thing was taken seriously all through.

Irreverent echo from the old Lambing Flat trouble, from camp across the gully:

> *Rule Britannia—Britannia rules the waves—*
> *No more Chinamen will enter Noo South Wales!*

and

Yankee doodle came to town
On a little pony—
Stick a feather in his cap,
And call him Macaroni!

All the camps seem to be singing tonight:

Ring the bell, watchman!
Ring! Ring! Ring!
Ring, for the good news
Is now on the wing!

Good lines, the introduction:

High on the belfry the old sexton stands,
Grasping the rope with his thin bony hands! . . .
Bonfires are blazing throughout the land . . .
Glorious and blessed tidings! Ring! Ring the bell!

Granny Mathews fails to coax her niece into the kitchen, but persuades her to sing inside. She is the girl who learnt *sub rosa* from the bad girl who sang "Madeline". Such as have them on instinctively take their hats off. Diggers, strolling past, halt at the first notes of the girl's voice, and stand like statues in the moonlight:

Shall we gather at the river,
Where bright angel feet have trod?
The beautiful—the beautiful river
That flows by the throne of God!

Diggers wanted to send that girl "Home", but Granny Mathews had the old-fashioned horror of any of her children becoming "public"—

Gather with the saints at the river,
That flows by the throne of God!

But it grows late, or rather, early. The "Eyetalians" go by in the frosty moonlight, from their last shift in the claim (for it is Saturday night), singing a litany.

"Get up on one end, Abe! Stand up all!" Hands are clasped across the kitchen table. Redclay, one of the last of the alluvial fields, has petered out, and the Roaring Days are dying. . . . The grand old song that is known all over the world; yet how many in ten thousand know more than one verse and the chorus? Let Peter McKenzie lead:

> *Should auld acquaintance be forgot,*
> *And never brought to min'?*

And hearts echo from far back in the past and across wide, wide seas:

> *Should auld acquaintance be forgot,*
> *And days o' lang syne?*

Now boys! all together!

> *For auld lang syne, my dear,*
>   *For auld lang syne,*
> *We'll tak' a cup o' kindness yet,*
>   *For auld lang syne.*
>
> *We twa hae run about the braes,*
>   *And pu'd the gowans fine;*
> *But we've wandered mony a weary foot,*
>   *Sin' auld lang syne.*

The world was wide then.

> *We twa hae paidl't i' the burn,*
>   *Frae mornin' sun till dine:*

the log fire seems to grow watery, for in wide, lonely Australia—

> *But seas between us braid hae roar'd,*
>   *Sin' auld lang syne.*

The kitchen grows dimmer, and the forms of the digger singers seemed suddenly vague and insubstantial, fading back rapidly through a misty veil. But the words ring strong and defiant through hard years:

> *And here's a hand, my trusty frien',*
>   *And gie's a grup o' thine;*
> *And we'll ta' a cup o' kindness yet,*
>   *For auld lang syne.*

And the nettles have been growing for over twenty years on the spot where Granny Mathews's big bark kitchen stood.

Two Sundowners

SHEEP-STATIONS in Australia are any distance from twenty to a hundred miles apart, to keep well within the boundaries of truth and the great pastoral country. Shearing at any one shed only lasts a few weeks in the year; the number of men employed is according to the size of the shed—from three to five men in the little bough-covered shed of the small "cockatoo", up to a hundred and fifty or two hundred hands all told in the big corrugated-iron machine shed of a pastoral company.

Shearing starts early up in northern Queensland, where you can get a "January shed"; and farther south, in February, March or April sheds, and so on down into New South Wales, where shearing often lasts over Christmas. Shearers travel from shed to shed; some go a travel season without getting a pen, and an unlucky shearer might ride or tramp for several seasons and never get hands in wool; and all this explains the existence of the "footman" with his swag and the horseman with his packhorse. They have a rough life, and the Australian shearers are certainly the most democratic and perhaps the most independent, intelligent and generous body of workmen in the world.

Shearers at a shed elect their own cook, pay him so much a head, and they buy their rations in the lump from the station store; and "travellers"—i.e., shearers and rouseabouts travelling for work—are invited, as a matter of course, to sit down to the shearers' table. Also a certain allowance of tea, sugar, flour or meat is still made to travellers at most western station stores; so it would be rather surprising if there weren't some who travelled on the game. The swagman loafer, or "bummer", times himself, especially in bad weather, to arrive at the shed just about sundown; he is then sure of "tea", shelter for the night, breakfast, and some tucker from the cook to take him on along the track. Brummy and Swampy were sundowners.

Swampy was a bummer born—and proud of it. Brummy had drifted down to loaferdom, and his nature was soured and his spirit revengeful against the world because of the memory of early years wasted at hard work and in being honest. Both were short and stout, and both had scrubby beards, but Brummy's beard was a dusty black and Swampy's fiery red—he indulged in a monkey-shave sometimes, but his lower face was mostly like a patch of coarse stubble with a dying hedge round it. They had travelled together for a long time. They seemed at times to hate each other with a murderous hatred, but they were too lazy to fight. Some-times they'd tramp side by side and growl at each other by the hour, other times they'd sulk for days; one would push on ahead and the other drop behind until there was a mile or two between them; but one always carried the billy or the sugar, or something that was necessary to the comfort of the other, so they'd come together at sundown. They had travelled together a long time, and perhaps that was why they hated each other. They often agreed to part and take different tracks, and sometimes they parted—for a while. They agreed in cadging, and cadged in turn. They carried a spare set of tucker-bags, and if, for instance, they were out of sugar and had plenty flour and tea, Brummy or Swampy would go to the store, boundary-rider's hut, or selector's, with the sugar-bag in his hand and the other bags in his shirt front on spec. He'd get the sugar first, and then, if it looked good enough, the flour-bag would come out, then the tea-bag. And before he left he'd remark casually that he and his mate hadn't had a smoke for two days. They never missed a chance. And when they'd cadged more tucker than they could comfortably carry, they'd camp for a day or two and eat it down. Sometimes they'd have as much as a pound of tobacco, all in little "borrowed" bits, cut from the sticks or cakes of honest travellers. They never missed a chance. If a stranger gave Swampy his cake of tobacco with instructions to "cut off a pipeful", Swampy would cut off as much as he thought judicious, talking to the stranger and watching his eye all the time, and hiding his palm as much as possible—and sometimes, when he knew he'd cut off more than he could cram into his pipe, he'd put his hand in his pocket for the pipe and drop some of the tobacco there. Then he'd hand the plug to his mate, engage the stranger in conversation and try to hold his eye or detract his attention from Brummy so as to give Brummy a chance of cutting off a couple of pipefuls, and, maybe, nicking off a corner of the cake and slipping it into his pocket. I once heard a bushman say that no one but a skunk would be guilty of this tobacco trick—that it is about the meanest trick a man could be capable of—*because it spoils the chances of the next hard-up swaggy who asks the victim for tobacco.*

When Brummy and Swampy came to a shed where shearing was in full swing, they'd inquire, first thing, and with some show of anxiety, if there was any chance of gettin' on; if the shed was full-handed they'd growl about hard times, wonder what the country was coming to; talk of their missuses and kids that they'd left in Sydney, curse the squatters and the Government, and, next morning, get a supply of rations from the cook and depart with looks of gloom. If, on the other hand, there was room in the shed for one or both of them, and the boss told them to go to work in the morning, they'd keep it quiet from the cook if possible, and depart, after breakfast, unostentatiously.

Sometimes, at the beginning of a drought, when the tall dead grass was like tinder for hundreds of miles and a carelessly-dropped match would set the whole country on fire, Swampy would strike a hard-faced squatter, manager, or overseer with a cold eye, and the conversation would be somewhat as follows:

Swampy: "Good day, boss!"

Boss (shortly): " 'Day."

Swampy: "Any chance of a job?"

Boss: "Naw. Got all I want and we don't start for a fortnight."

Swampy: "Can I git a bit o' meat?"

Boss: "Naw! Don't kill till Saturday."

Swampy: "Pint o' flour?"

Boss: "Naw. Short ourselves."

Swampy: "Bit o' tea or sugar, boss?"

Boss: "Naw—what next?"

Swampy: "Bit o' baccer, boss. Ain't had a smoke for a week."

Boss: "Naw. Ain't got enough for meself till the wagon comes out."

Swampy: "Ah, well! It's hot, ain't it, boss?"

Boss: "Yes—it's hot."

Swampy: "Country very dry?"

Boss: "Yes. Looks like it."

Swampy: "A fire 'ud be very bad just now?"

Boss: "Eh?"

Swampy: "Yes. Now I'm allers very careful with matches an' fire when I'm on the track."

Boss: "Are yer?"

Swampy: "Yes. I never lights a fire near the grass—allers in the middle of the track—it's the safest place yer can get. An' I allers puts the fire out afore I leaves the camp. If there ain't no water ter spare I covers the ashes with dirt. An' some fellers are so careless with matches lightin' their pipes." (Reflective pause.)

Boss: "Are they?"

Swampy: "Yes. Now, when I lights me pipe on the track in dry weather I allers rubs the match head up an' drops it in the dust. I never drops a burnin' match. But some travellers is so careless. A chap might light his pipe an' fling the match away without thinkin' an' the match might fall in a dry tuft, an'—there yer are!" (with a wave of his arms). "Hundreds of miles o' grass gone an' thousands o' sheep starvin'. Some fellers is so careless—they never thinks. . . . An' what's more, they don't care if they burn the whole country."

Boss (scratching his head reflectively): "Ah—umph!—You can go up to the store and get a bit of tucker. The storekeeper might let yer have a bit o' tobacco."

On one occasion, when they were out of flour and meat, Brummy and Swampy came across two other pilgrims camped on a creek, who were also out of flour and meat. One of them had tried a surveyors' camp a little farther down, but without success. The surveyors' cook had said that he was short of flour and meat himself. Brummy tried him—no luck. Then Swampy said *he'd* go and have a try. As luck would have it, the surveyors' cook was just going to bake; he had got the flour out in the dish, put in the salt and baking-powder, mixed it up, and had gone to the creek for a billy of water when Swampy arrived. While the cook was gone Swampy slipped the flour out of the dish into his bag, *wiped* the dish, set it down again, and planted the bag behind a tree at a little distance. Then he stood waiting, holding a spare empty bag in his hand. When the cook came back he glanced at the dish, lowered the billy of water slowly to the ground, scratched his head, and looked at the dish again in a puzzled way.

"Blanked if I didn't think I got that flour out!" he said.

"What's that, mate?" asked Swampy.

"Why! I could have sworn I got the flour out in the dish and mixed it before I went for the water," said the cook, staring at the dish again. "It's rum what tricks your memory plays on you sometimes."

"Yes," said Swampy, showing interest, while the cook got some more flour out into the dish from a bag in the back of the tent. "It is strange. I've done the same thing meself. I suppose it's the heat that makes us all a bit off at times."

"Do you cook, then?" asked the surveyors' cook.

"Well, yes. I've done a good bit of it in me time; but it's about played out. I'm after stragglers now." (Stragglers are stray sheep missed in the general muster and found about the out paddocks and shorn after the general shearing.)

They had a yarn and Swampy "bit the cook's ear" for a "bit o' meat an' tea an' sugar", not forgetting "a handful of flour if yer can spare it".

"Sorry," said the cook, "but I can only let you have about a pint. We're very short ourselves."

"Oh, that's all right!" said Swampy, as he put the stuff into his spare bags. "Thank you! Good day!"

"Good day," said the cook.

The cook went on with his work and Swampy departed, catching up the bag of flour from behind the tree as he passed it, and keeping the clump of timber well between him and the surveyors' camp, lest the cook should glance round, and, noticing the increased bulk of his load, get some new ideas concerning mental aberration.

Nearly every bushman has at least one superstition, or notion, that lasts his time—as nearly every bushman has at least one dictionary word which lasts him all his life. Brummy had a gloomy notion— Lord knows how he got it!—that he should 'a' gone on the boards if his people hadn't been so ignorant. He reckoned that he had the face and cut of an actor, could mimic any man's voice, and had wonderful control over his features. They came to a notoriously "hungry" station, where there was a Scottish manager and store-keeper. Brummy went up to "Government House" in his own proper person, had a talk with the storekeeper, spoke of a sick mate, and got some flour and meat. They camped down the creek, and next morning Brummy started to shave himself.

"Whatever are you a-doin' of, Brummy?" gasped Swampy in great astonishment.

"Wait and see," growled Brummy, with awful impressiveness, as if he were going to cut Swampy's throat after he'd finished shaving. He shaved off his beard and whiskers, put on a hat and coat belonging to Swampy, changed his voice, dropped his shoulders, and went limping up to the station on a game leg. He saw the cook and got some brownie, a bit of cooked meat and a packet of baking-powder. Then he saw the storekeeper and approached the tobacco question. Sandy looked at him and listened with some slight show of interest, then he said:

"Oh that's all right now! But ye needn't ha' troublt shavin' yer beard—the cold weather's comin' on! An' yer mate's duds don't suit ye—they're too sma'; an' yer game leg doesn't fit ye either—it takes a lot o' practice. Ha'ye got any tea an' sugar?"

Brummy must have touched something responsive in that old Scot somewhere, but *his* lack of emotion upset Brummy somewhat, or else an old deep-rooted superstition had been severely shaken. Anyway he let Swampy do the cadging for several days thereafter.

But one bad season they were very hard up indeed—even for Brummy and Swampy. They'd tramped a long hungry track, and had only met a few wretched jackeroos, driven out of the cities by hard times, and tramping hopelessly west. They were out of tobacco, and their trousers were so hopelessly gone behind that when they went to cadge at a place where there was a woman they were moved to back and sidle and edge away again—and neither Brummy nor Swampy was over fastidious in matters of dress or personal appearance. It was absolutely necessary to earn a pound or two, so they decided to go to work for a couple of weeks. It wouldn't hurt them, and then there was the novelty of it.

They struck West-o'-Sunday Station, and the boss happened to want a rouseabout to pick up wool and sweep the floor for the shearers.

"I can put *one* of you on," he said. "Fix it up between yourselves and go to work in the morning."

Brummy and Swampy went apart to talk it over.

"Look here, Brum, old man," said Swampy, with great heartiness, "we've been mates for a long while now, an' shared an' shared alike. You've allers acted straight to me an' I want to do the fair thing by you. *I* don't want to stand in *your* light. You take the job an' I'll be satisfied with a pair of pants out of it and a bit o' tobacco now an' agen. There yer are! I can't say no fairer than that."

"Yes," said Brummy, resentfully, "an' you'll always be throwin' it up to me afterwards that I done you out of a job!"

"I'll swear I won't," said Swampy, hurriedly. "But since you're so blasted touchy and suspicious about it, *you* take this job an' I'll take the next that turns up. How'll that suit you?"

Brummy thought resentfully.

"Look here," he said presently; "let's settle it and have done with this damned sentimental tommy-rot. I'll tell you what I'll do—I'll give you the job and take my chance. The boss might want another man tomorrow. Now, are you satisfied?"

But Swampy didn't look grateful or happy.

"Well," growled Brummy, "of all the —— I ever travelled with you're the ——! What do you want anyway? What'll satisfy you? That's all I want to know. Hey?—can't yer speak?"

"Let's toss up for it," said Swampy, sulkily.

"All right," said Brummy, with a big oath, and he felt in his pocket for two old pennies he had. But Swampy had got a suspicion somehow that one of those pennies had two heads on it, and he wasn't sure that the other hadn't two tails—also, he suspected Brummy of some skill in palming, so he picked up a chip from the woodheap, spat on it, and spun it into the air. "Sing out!" he cried. "Wet or dry?"

"Dry," said Brummy, promptly. He had a theory that the wet side of the chip, being presumably heaviest, was more likely to fall downwards; but this time it was "wet" up three times in succession. Brummy ignored Swampy's hand thrown out in hearty congratulation; and next morning he went to work in the shed. Swampy camped down the river, and Brummy supplied him with a cheap pair of moleskin trousers, tucker and tobacco. The shed cut out within three weeks and the two sundowners took the track again, Brummy with two pounds odd in his pocket—he having negotiated his cheque at the shed.

But now there was suspicion, envy, and distrust in the hearts of those two wayfarers. Brummy was now a bloated capitalist, and proud, and anxious to get rid of Swampy—at least Swampy thought so. He thought that the least that Brummy might have done was to have shared the "stuff" with him.

"Look here, Brummy," he said reproachfully, "we've shared and shared alike, and——"

"We never shared money," said Brummy, decidedly.

"Do you think I want yer blasted money?" retorted Swampy, indignantly. "When did I ever ask yer for a sprat? Tell me that!"

"You wouldn't have got it if you had asked," said Brummy, uncompromisingly. "Look here!" with vehemence. "Didn't I keep yer in tobacco and buy yer gory pants? What are you naggin' about anyway?"

"Well," said Swampy, "all I was goin' to say was that yer might let me carry one of them quids in case you lost one—yer know you're careless and lose things; or in case anything happened to you."

"I ain't going to lose it—if that's all that's fretting you," said Brummy, "and there ain't nothing going to happen to me—and don't you forget it."

"That's all the thanks I get for givin' yer my gory job," said Swampy, savagely. "I won't be sich a soft fool agen, I can tell yer."

Brummy was silent, and Swampy dropped behind. He brooded darkly, and it's a bad thing for a man to brood in the bush. He was reg'lar disgusted with Brummy. He'd allers acted straight to him, and Brummy had acted like a "cow". He'd stand it no longer; but he'd have some satisfaction. He wouldn't be a fool. If Brummy was mean skunk enough to act to a mate like that, Swampy would be even with him; he would wait till Brummy was asleep, collar the stuff, and clear. It was his job, anyway, and the money was his by rights. He'd have his rights.

Brummy, who carried the billy, gave Swampy a long tramp before he camped and made a fire. They had tea in silence, and smoked moodily apart until Brummy turned in. They usually slept on the ground, with a few leaves under them, or on the sand where there was any, each wrapped in his own blankets, and with their spare clothes, or rags rather, for pillows. Presently Swampy turned in and pretended to sleep, but he lay awake watching, and listening to Brummy's breathing. When he thought it was safe he moved cautiously and slipped his hand under Brummy's head, but Brummy's old pocket-book—in which he carried some dirty old letters in a woman's handwriting—was not there. All next day Swampy watched Brummy sharply every time he put his hands into his pockets, to try and find out in which pocket he kept his money. Brummy seemed very cheerful and sociable, even considerate, to his mate all day, and Swampy pretended to be happy. They yarned more than they had done for many a day. Brummy was a heavy sleeper, and that night Swampy went over him carefully and felt all his pockets, but without success. Next day Brummy seemed in high spirits—they were nearing Bourke, where they intended to loaf round the pubs for a week or two. On the third night Swampy waited till about midnight, and then searched Brummy, every inch of him he could get at, and tickled him with a straw of grass till he turned over, and ran his hands over the other side of him, and over his feet (Brummy slept with his socks on), and looked in his boots, and in the billy and in the tucker-bags, and felt in every tuft of grass round the camp, and under every bush, and down a hollow stump, and up a hollow log: but there was no pocket-book. Brummy couldn't have lost the money and kept it dark—he'd have gone back to look for it at once. Perhaps he'd thrown away the book and sewn the money in his clothes somewhere. Swampy crept back to him and felt the lining of his hat, and was running his hand over Brummy's chest when Brummy suddenly started to snore, and Swampy desisted without loss of time. He crept back to bed, breathing short, and thought hard. It struck him that there was something aggressive about that snore. He began to suspect that Brummy was up to his little game, and it pained him.

Next morning Brummy was decidedly frivolous. At any other time Swampy would have put it down to a "touch o' the sun", but now he felt a growing conviction that Brummy knew what he'd been up to the last three nights, and the more he thought of it the more it pained him—till at last he could stand it no longer.

"Look here, Brummy," he said frankly, "where the hell do you keep that flamin' stuff o' yourn? I been tryin' to git at it ever since we left West-o'-Sunday."

"I know you have, Swampy," said Brummy, affectionately—as if he considered that Swampy had done his best in the interests of mateship.

"I *knowed* yer knowed!" exclaimed Swampy, triumphantly. "But where the blazes did yer put it?"

"Under *your* head, Swampy, old man," said Brummy, cheerfully.

Swampy was hurt now. He commented in the language that used to be used by the bullock-punchers of the good days as they pranced up and down by their teams and lammed into the bullocks with saplings and crowbars, and called on them to lift a heavy load out of a bog in the bed of a muddy creek.

"Never mind, Swampy!" said Brummy, soothingly, as his mate paused and tried to remember worse oaths. "It wasn't your fault."

But they parted at Bourke. Swampy had allers acted straight ter

185

Brummy—share 'n' share alike. He'd do as much for a mate as any other man, an' put up with as much from a mate. He had put up with a lot from Brummy: he'd picked him up on the track and learned him all he knowed; Brummy would have starved many a time if it hadn't been for Swampy; Swampy had learned him how to battle. He'd stick to Brummy yet, but he couldn't stand ingratitude. He hated low cunnin' an' suspicion, and when a gory mate got suspicious of his own old mate and wouldn't trust him, an' took to plantin' his crimson money—it was time to leave him.